DESIGNING WITH LEATHER AND FUR

Hearthside Press, Incorporated, Publishers
Great Neck, New York 11021

DESIGNING
WITH
LEATHER
AND
FUR

By Mary Patton

DEDICATION

To Jim for tolerance above and beyond the call of duty: and to the memory of my Aunt Georgie who kept sticking crayons, pastels and paintbrushes in my hands from the time I was 6 years old.

ACKNOWLEDGEMENTS

My special thanks to my husband, James Patton, for the black and white photography; to Lynn Dorman for financial assistance; and to Eileen Ferado for her assistance in preparing the text of this book.

I also wish to thank my Uncle Farrington Daniels, Daina and Challis Vupulis, and the people at Gene Hacker's Camera Shop (especially Vermon Rudd) in Hackensack, N.J. for their advice and aid with the photography; Cally Koontz of Cally Furs, Haworth, N.J., for her instruction in fur techniques; Tom Baeli from the Bergen Mall Shoe Repair Shop in Paramus, N.J., for technical advice; Mac of Mac Leathers at 424 Broome St., New York City, for his information on types of leathers and for his advice so freely and pleasantly given on anything about leather; and last but not least, my parents, Mr. and Mrs. Robert W. Swartwood for constant encouragement and assistance while I pursued my art career.

CONTENTS

Introduction

An animal skin was, no doubt, our primitive ancestors very first fashion. It must have served him well to persist in favor through the millenias. More and more ways were found to work, wear, color, decorate, shape and utilize skins. And they served endlessly: from primitive water bags to wall decorations for the cave man, right up to the shoulder bag and mini-skirt of today. Some form or other of leather crafting was found all around the world. And, inevitably, leather decorating developed into a fine art. Magnificent examples of tooled or embossed leathers are to be found in museums everywhere.

But, right here and now, we are witnessing a resurgence of leather in both fashion and in our modern "caves"—with no end in sight for the imaginative and interesting effects possible. No longer are leathers decorated only by standard methods of tooling. Exciting things are happening to leather because today's uninhibited craftsman are experimenting with paints, inks, marking pens, studs, appliqué, stitching, weaving and knotting. The result is both beautiful and practical. Practical, because paints and findings left from other projects, can be used in your leather work.

There will be simple projects to begin with (like the very easy suede choker). New skills and techniques will be introduced with each new project. However, not all the projects are of leather: techniques for working the new man-made leather-like or fur-like materials are included too.

Step-by-step directions are given for the beginner—but as you develop skill in working with leather and suede, it is my sincere hope that you will add your own creative designs to make an item uniquely your own.

1. Leather Now

Leather used in the United States today by individual craftsmen comes mainly from three animals; the cow and calf, the sheep and lamb, and the goat and kid.

Animal pelts are classified according to size. Pelts from large animals such as cows and horses are called hides. Those from the same but not fully mature animals are called kips, and pelts from small animals like goats, sheep, calves and rabbits are called skins.

Before the pelt can be used by the craftsman or manufacturer it must be tanned, a process meant primarily to prevent decomposition. This can be done simply by drying or salting, but these processes tend to make the pelt stiff and unmanageable. More complicated tanning procedures were devised not only to clean the pelt more thoroughly, but at the same time, make it tougher and more pliable.

There are two basic types of tanning which are most frequently used; bark or vegetable-tanning and chrome or mineral-tanning. Both processes involve soaking the pelts in solutions. Because bark or vegetable-tanning is done with plant extracts, the solutions used are naturally weaker and therefore the entire process takes a long time (sometimes as long as six months). As stronger and more potent solutions can be made from minerals, chrome-tanning takes only a few hours to complete. Bark-tanning produces a very firm leather while chrome-tanning produces a very soft leather.

Although the leather is somewhat softer after tanning than it is after salting or drying, it is still rather stiff and must be softened further by rubbing greases and oils into it. Then the leather may be processed in a number of other ways.

It may be put through machines which split the hide into several layers to produce skins of a uniform thickness. Just how thick a layer of hide will be, is determined by how the leather will be used. It can be dyed another color; made into suede by passing it between rough rollers which rip the fibers; glazed with glass rollers; embossed with another grain or design by pressing with a heated carved plate; polished with roller brushes to obtain a high luster or hand-grained to bring out the natural grain.

Listed below are various kinds of leathers and their characteristics. Use it for deciding which leather to choose for a specific project.

REAL LEATHER AND SUEDE

COW SIDES: Leather made from half of a whole hide by cutting along the backbone; comes in different weights and thicknesses; does not stretch easily; when vegetable-tanned, it may be tooled; cowhides can be processed to look like hides from other animals.

LATIGO: Sometimes called rawhide; is chrome-tanned cowhide; durable but flexible; stretches very little; used commercially for work boots and heavy handbags.

SPLIT COWHIDE: Called split because one hide is split into three or more separate skins (known as skiving); can be purchased as smooth leather; but usually refers to suede splits; very little stretch.

REVERSIBLE COWHIDE: One side is suede finished the other is leather; stretches easily.

CALFSKIN: Naturally thinner and softer because the animal is younger; when vegetable-tanned it can be tooled; can be purchased with the hair on.

LAMBSKIN: Obtained from both lambs and sheep; refers to skins without the hair; as leather, it is very thin; as suede, it is thin, has a short nap and does not shed; both stretch very little.

SHEEPSKIN: Wooly because the hair is left on; the hair is sometimes combed and bleached (combing makes the hair seem long and fluffy, bleaching whitens the hair); sometimes dyed brown on the ends; when left natural the hair is yellowish in color and tightly curled; can also be purchased sheared to various lengths.

CABRETTA: Sheepskin without the hair; wrinkled texture; very soft; stretches easily.

CHAMOIS: Was once obtained from an animal called a chamois; now usually a suede-finished sheepskin; short suede nap; feels like cloth; stretches excessively.

GOAT AND KIDSKIN: The adult goatskin is usually processed to resemble the skin of the younger animal; usually a very soft, smooth, lightweight leather; does not stretch much; can be purchased with the hair on.

MOROCCAN LEATHER: Obtained from a goat; processed to have a very small pebble grain and slightly shiny surface; does not stretch easily.

PIGSKIN: Pinhole grain. Two types: 1. carpincho: the hide of a South American capybara (a water rodent); fine, soft-grained. 2. wild boar skin; when bark-tanned it is hard and grainy when chrome-tanned, it has a very short suede nap and a barely noticeable grain; tough and durable. Domestic pigskin is rarely used as it is too tough to be of any use.

DEERSKIN: Soft, fine wrinkle-grained leather; stretches; falls like cloth when used to make garments.

BUCKSKIN: Wrinkle-grained; heavier and stiffer than latigo; can be processed to be softer but is hard to find.

ELK: Soft, wrinkle-grained; heavier than deerskin; suitable for heavy clothing.

ANTELOPE: Small pinhole grain; much softer than pigskin which also has a pinhole grain; feels like suede; thinner than elk; wears well for outer jackets.

OTHERS: Alligator, camel, dolphin, elephant, frog, horse, kangaroo, lizard, mule, ostrich, seal, shark, snake, walrus, water buffalo.

Many of these skins will not be found in local leather shops. Real antelope skins are imported, obviously not easy to catch, and expensive. Elephant hides take at least 6 months to tan. And, as many conscientious ecologists will agree, the balance of nature is more important than private possession of a seal or alligator skin. Other skins, I would guess, are reserved for manufacturers, probably even before the animal is captured.

When you enter a leather shop, you may be overwhelmed at what seems to be so many different kinds of leather. Actually, you are looking at many varieties of cowhides processed into suedes or embossed to resemble antelope or perhaps other more exotic skins. After you look around you'll be convinced that you can get any effect you may want from one kind of hide—cowhide, in all its guises.

SHOPPING FOR LEATHER

No matter where you live, a few hints might make purchasing the leather a little easier.

1. If you're not sure that a specific piece of leather is suitable for your project ask the shopkeeper to help you choose correctly.

2. Do not expect a perfect piece of leather—there's no such thing. But,

do try to choose pieces with the fewest flaws, holes or scars, or pieces that will allow you to work around the flaws.

3. Hold the piece up to the light to detect very small holes.

4. If more than one piece is needed be sure to match the color by buying them all at once. Each dye lot (of red, for instance) results in a slightly different shade.

5. Rub your hand back and forth over dyed suede. If the dye comes off on your hand it will certainly come off on your clothes, especially when you sweat. Especially reds, maroons, red-browns and some purples should be tested this way.

6. Most split suedes shed, but if it really comes off on your hands or clothing while handling it, choose another piece.

7. Take your pattern with you and lay it out on the pieces you've chosen to be sure you have enough. Very often the same color will not be available the next day.

8. For large articles of clothing the pattern should usually be laid in one direction. The more the leather stretches the more this is necessary. With suede the color changes when the nap does not run in the same direction. Sometimes the difference is so negligible as to be unimportant. But take this into account when purchasing.

9. It takes lots of practice to be able to recognize different types of leather. Even the experienced leather craftsman can become confused because very often a cowhide has been processed to resemble another animal skin so successfully that it's impossible to tell the real from the copy. Don't let this bother you; just be sure you get the proper type of leather for the project you're making.

10. Leather is sold by the square foot and the size is marked on the wrong side and at the tail end of each piece. They'll be marked 6, 6^1, 6^2, 6^3 which means 6 feet, $6\frac{1}{4}$ feet, 6 2/4 ($\frac{1}{2}$) feet, or $6\frac{3}{4}$ feet.

11. Leather thickness is noted in terms of ounces. One ounce leather is 1/64 inch thick. Eight ounce leather is 8/64 or $\frac{1}{8}$-inch thick.

12. There is a formula you can use to estimate the square feet required:

36-INCH WIDE MATERIAL

a. Multiply the yardage by 9 (i.e. If the pattern calls for 5 yards— $5 \times 9 = 45$)

b. Multiply this answer by 15% to find the waste allowance (45 $\times$ .15 = 6.65)

c. Add the required yardage to this number ($6.65 + 45 = 51.65$ square feet)

FOR 54-INCH FABRIC

Multiply the yardage by 13 and repeat steps b and c accordingly.
13. Division of hides (fig. 1), a split hide (fig. 2).

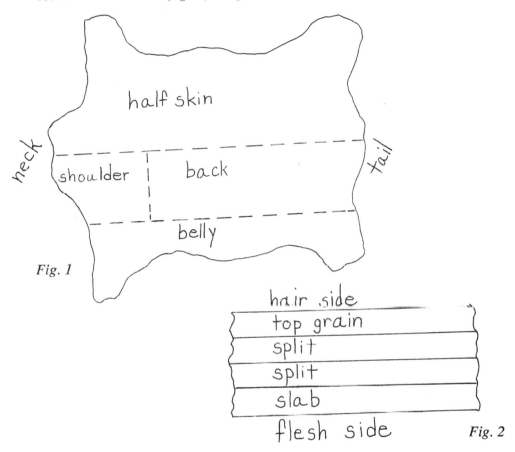

Fig. 1

Fig. 2

FAKE LEATHERS AND SUEDES

Fake leathers are made from vinyl or heat embossed double knits. The vinyl leathers are crisp and firm while the embossed double knits are soft, pliable and very stretchable. They must therefore be lined when made into garments that will cover parts of the body that bend, like knees and elbows.

Like leather, once a hole is made in these fabrics it's there to stay. Tape the pattern to the wrong side or use pins within the seam allowance only.

Vinyl can not be pressed or dry-cleaned and because it is a stiff fabric, wide darts and curved seams should be avoided. Vinyl doesn't stretch to fit your form as leather does, so be sure your pattern fits correctly before cutting. Gluing all seams open and topstitching will help flatten seams, hems and edges. Avoid sharp corners because they don't turn neatly. Interfacing is not necessary. Buttonholes are easy to work because the fabrics are firm. Bulk should be eliminated by finishing areas like waistlines with grosgrain ribbon instead of facing with leather fabric.

Knitted leathers must be faced, but, because of their pliability, they can be worked as easily as fabric. They can be washed or dry-cleaned. Keep in mind their stretchability at all times. Do not use them for slacks or tight sleeves.

Fake suedes are usually bonded and if they are of heavy quality tend to be stiff-looking. When thinner, they do not have the weight real suede has which is an important factor in the way the finished garment hangs. Cut the pattern pieces in one direction and interface for weight.

Whenever working on the right side of any of these fabrics use brown paper strips to protect the cloth and to help it move through the machine easily.

Sew with long stitches and use a fine or medium needle from size 11 to 16 and heavy-duty mercerized thread. Short stitches, especially on vinyl, may rip the fabric. Fake leathers or suede can be used to create most of the items in this book if you keep in mind these special techniques.

CARE, CLEANING AND STORING OF LEATHER AND SUEDE

LEATHER

Leathers can occasionally be wiped clean with a damp cloth if, for instance, something sticky has spilled on it. Never use water to clean leathers that have been decorated with water-base paints or inks.

Saddle soap can be used to clean all leather surfaces, and leather balm may be used to deep-clean smooth leathers.

It is best to condition and to add protective coatings to leather before wearing them. Leather should be conditioned at least two times a year to extend the life of the garment.

Soft leathers can be pressed with a dry iron on a warm setting. Brown paper or a pressing cloth must be placed over the leather to protect it from the direct heat of the iron.

When storing unused hides, never fold them. Whenever possible lay them out flat. If this cannot be done, wrap the hides carefully around long cardboard tubes, flattening and smoothing them as you go. Have the right sides of two skins facing each other. Store these rolls on their sides. Do not stand them up on end. The thicker tooling cowhide will not roll up into tight rolls. Simply roll them as tightly as possible and lay them on their sides, also. Roll them with the right side inside to keep it from getting damaged.

To avoid mildew, do not store any leather or suede in damp places.

Finished leather garments should be hung up when not in use. I even hang my belts up to avoid fold marks.

Suede

Suede will liven up if you brush up the nap under steam, with a medium or soft bristle brush.

If food or solid moist material has fallen onto suede do not wipe it off until it dries. When dried, brush it off with a medium or hard bristle brush. If necessary, steam and brush it. And if that fails, remove shiny spots by filing them off with a fine emery board. If the spots on the suede are due to wear, nothing will help.

Water or liquids should be blotted up immediately. Do not rub or wipe them off because you'll spread the damage. When as much as possible of the liquid is blotted up, allow suede to dry and then brush up the nap. Again, steaming and filing may be useful.

It's not advisable to press suede, but if you must do it, use one or more layers of terry cloth to protect it and press with a steam iron.

There are no guarantees with suede so handle and wear it carefully.

HOW TO FIND MATERIALS IN YOUR AREA

For all leather craftsmen who live in small towns or no towns at all and who have difficulty obtaining supplies, there are a number of mail order houses listed in the back of this book. If you would like to see if there are any additional mail order houses nearer to you, check your yellow pages.

No matter where you live there's a very simple procedure for finding sources of supply close by. First, check your local yellow pages and the yellow pages of the nearest city. Leather sources may be found under *leather* or *leather scraps* and then possibly under *leather findings* and *art and crafts suppliers*. Tools, dyes and decorative hardware will also be found under the last two general headings. Other supplies such as needles, Pellon or threads may be found in notions and trimming shops or departments.

Personally, I prefer to save myself a lot of leg work and time by calling the establishment and finding out if they carry what I need and if they'll sell me the amount I need. Many shops which advertise selling to wholesale dealers, only, will also sell single pieces to anyone walking in off the street.

TOOLS FOR LEATHER AND SUEDE

AWL: Used for marking distances, making holes, enlarging holes, or piercing (fig. 3).

LEATHER KNIFE: Used for cutting heavy leather (fig. 4).

MAT KNIFE: Used to cut through suede, paper, cardboard (fig. 5).

FURRIER'S KNIFE: Used to cut fur. Because of its thinness, it is easier to control (fig. 6).

REVOLVING PUNCH: Used for cutting round holes. It has 6 different sizes of holes (fig. 7).

STITCHING CHISEL: Used to punch evenly-spaced holes in lightweight leather or suede (fig. 8).

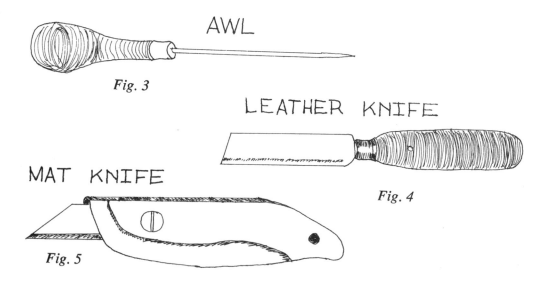

AWL

Fig. 3

LEATHER KNIFE

Fig. 4

MAT KNIFE

Fig. 5

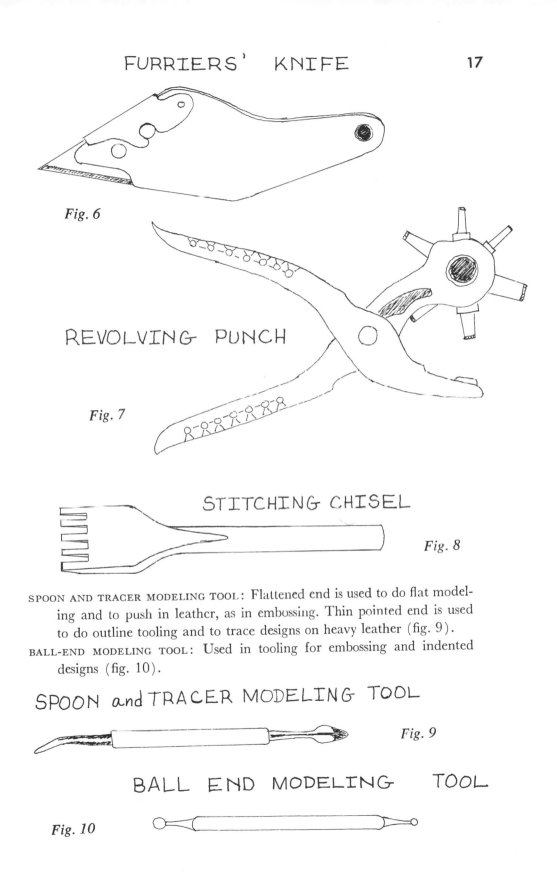

Fig. 6

REVOLVING PUNCH

Fig. 7

STITCHING CHISEL

Fig. 8

SPOON AND TRACER MODELING TOOL: Flattened end is used to do flat modeling and to push in leather, as in embossing. Thin pointed end is used
to do outline tooling and to trace designs on heavy leather (fig. 9).

BALL-END MODELING TOOL: Used in tooling for embossing and indented
designs (fig. 10).

SPOON and TRACER MODELING TOOL

Fig. 9

BALL END MODELING TOOL

Fig. 10

STAMPING TOOLS: Available in a variety of designs. Each tool has one design. The tool cuts the design into the leather (figs. 11 and 12).

SWIVEL KNIFE: Used to cut leather in carved or incised lines (fig. 13).

SOLDERING IRON: Used to burn designs on leather (fig. 14).

ROUGHING TOOL: Used to rip and roughen leather surfaces so that when glue is used, the surfaces will bond together firmly (fig. 15).

MALLET: Made from rawhide, wood, rubber or fiber. Used for striking stamps (fig. 16).

EYELET SETTER: Used to flatten and set eyelets (fig. 17).

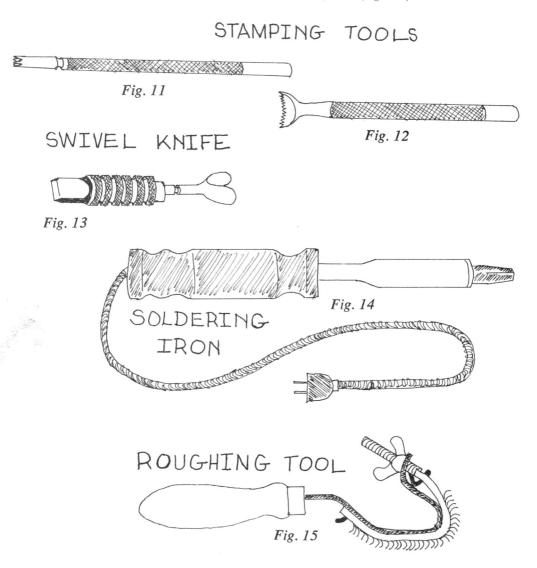

STAMPING TOOLS

Fig. 11

Fig. 12

SWIVEL KNIFE

Fig. 13

SOLDERING IRON

Fig. 14

ROUGHING TOOL

Fig. 15

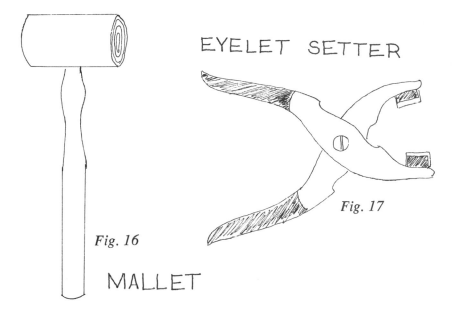

EYELET SETTER

Fig. 17

Fig. 16

MALLET

COMPASS: Used to lay out circles, ovals and spaces. May also be used to space stitches (fig. 18).

GLOVER'S NEEDLES: Used in sewing fur and lightweight leathers. They have a 3-sided sharp point and come in various sizes (fig. 19).

HARNESS NEEDLES: Used in hand sewing. They have a blunt point (fig. 20).

COMPASS

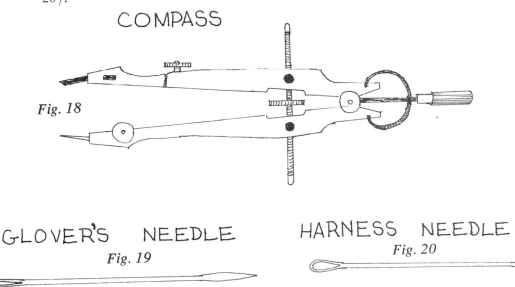

Fig. 18

GLOVER'S NEEDLE
Fig. 19

HARNESS NEEDLE
Fig. 20

Note: Good tools can make the work faster, neater and easier. However, you often can improvise. For instance, an awl or an ice pick can be used to make several sizes of holes. Sandpaper may make a satisfactory roughing tool and cutting can be done with a razor or an ordinary scissors that is large enough to handle the job. For many of my projects, a revolving punch or awl and a heavy duty scissors are all the tools needed. Buy only those tools required by your project.

Sharpening Tools

You can use your tools a long time before they'll need sharpening. If you plan doing very much leather work with the tools used in this book you will occasionally need to sharpen them.

When sharpening any tool, the sharp edge of the blade should rest on the sharpening stone or device at its original beveled angle. If this is not done, there is a good chance that you'll make it worse rather than improve it.

All tools with simple flat blades are sharpened on an oilstone which comes with one rough side and one smoother side. For any blade, first apply a few drops of 3-in-1 oil to the middle of the stone. The leather knife, scissors, awl, thonging chisel and swivel knife can all be sharpened on an oilstone. Always clean the stone after each use by wiping it with a soft cloth.

Sharpen all tools on the roughest side first and then refine by repeating the process on the smoother side.

LEATHER KNIFE, THONGING CHISEL, SWIVEL KNIFE: Holding the blade against the stone at the naturally beveled edge of the blade, push the cutting edge away from you while applying pressure. Sharpen both edges if the tool has two. Polish the swivel knife by repeating this process on a crocus cloth, which is available at hardware stores (figs. 21-23).

Sharpening Leather Knife

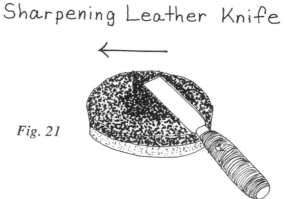

Fig. 21

Sharpening Stitching Chisel

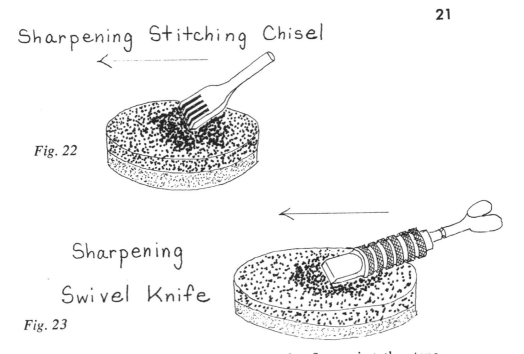

Fig. 22

Sharpening

Swivel Knife

Fig. 23

AWL: With the point and side of its slanted edge flat against the stone, revolve the awl between your fingers while pulling it across the stone (fig. 24).

REVOLVING PUNCH: To sharpen the cutting tubes, use a medium-grain emery cloth looped around one tube and pull it back and forth (fig. 25). The anvil (which is the flat surface that the cutting tubes hit when in use) may become rough. File it smooth with a fine steel file.

MALLET: If your mallet becomes very worn, saw off a thin slice and sand it smooth.

Sharpening Awl

Fig. 24

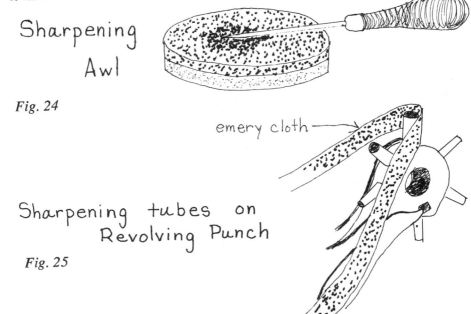

emery cloth

Sharpening tubes on Revolving Punch

Fig. 25

FINDINGS AND DECORATIVE HARDWARE

DECORATIVE NAILS: Nails with a decorative head. Both nail and head vary in size and ornateness (fig. 26).

UPHOLSTERY AND CARPET TACKS: Flat-headed steel nails with a thick shaft and an angled pointed tip (fig. 27).

EYELETS: Used to reinforce and strengthen holes for laces to go through. Especially helpful in areas where lacing must be frequently loosened and tightened (fig. 28).

SPOTS: Decorative metal spots attached by inserting the prongs through the leather and bending the prongs in, (fig. 29).

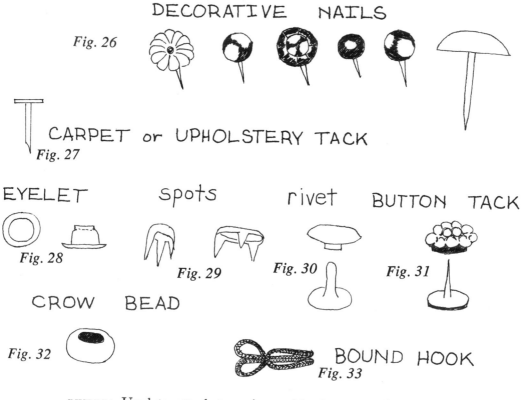

DECORATIVE NAILS

Fig. 26

CARPET or UPHOLSTERY TACK
Fig. 27

EYELET   spots   rivet   BUTTON TACK

Fig. 28   *Fig. 29*   *Fig. 30*   *Fig. 31*

CROW BEAD

Fig. 32

BOUND HOOK
Fig. 33

RIVETS: Used to attach two pieces of leather or as decoration on a single thickness (fig. 30).

BUTTON TACKS: Used to attach two pieces of leather while also being decorative (fig. 31).

CROW BEADS: Plastic or glass. The hole in this bead is large enough to allow a leather or suede thong to go through it (fig. 32).

BOUND HOOKS: Wire bound with cloth. They come in varying sizes and can be bent (fig. 33).

SNAPS

There are four parts to a snap; the cap and eyelet, the spring and post (fig. 34). Different kinds of snaps vary slightly. Whichever you choose, be sure you purchase the appropriate snap setter. A snap setter consists of two parts (fig. 35), and although the parts do not look alike the setting procedure is basically the same. If you understand one type, you can easily figure out any other.

Punch a hole in the leather. Fit the cap in the hole from the right side to the wrong side. Place the eyelet on the cap's post. Place the cap in the concave portion of the die. This will protect it from denting. Place the steel rod or bodkin in the eyelet portion. If it does not fit snugly, center it carefully and hold it there (fig. 36). Hit the end of the steel rod firmly with a heavy large-headed hammer. Do the hammering on a concrete floor or a very sturdy work bench as any other surface tends to give under the pressure and does not successfully set the snap.

Punch a hole in the leather opposite the cap and eyelet's hole. Push the post portion of the snap through this hole from the right side of the leather to the wrong side. Place the spring portion on the post (fig. 37). Turn the die over. This side is flat and makes a good bed for this portion of the snap. Fit the rod in the spring portion and hammer to set.

snap setter

Fig. 35

cap   eyelet   post   spring

Fig. 34

die   bodkin

24

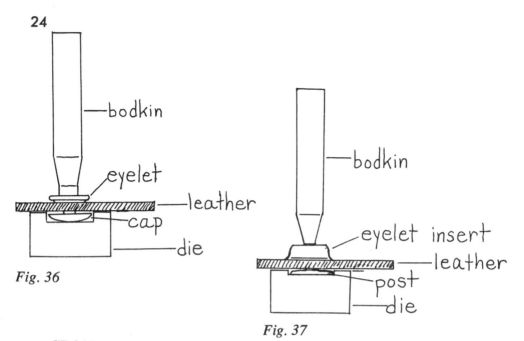

Fig. 36

Fig. 37

GROMMETS

A grommet is a two part finding used to line and reinforce holes. They're made for larger holes than eyelets would fit. The two parts of the grommet is the grommet itself and the washer (fig. 38).

Punch a hole slightly smaller than the grommet's hole. Put the grommet on the die. The die must be the correct size for the size grommet being used. Place the leather over the grommet. Place the washer on top of this, convex side up. Place the pointed end of the grommet setter into the grommet (fig. 39). Strike with a heavy, large-headed hammer.

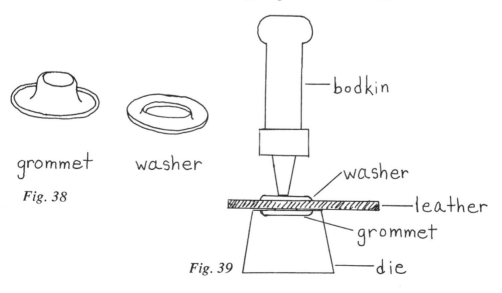

Fig. 38

Fig. 39

2. Leather How

These are general directions for working leather; detailed instructions are also given under each individual project.

1. Always make any pen or chalk marks on the wrong side of the hide.

2. When cutting patterns tape the pattern pieces to the wrong side of the hide or pin the pattern within the seam allowance only.

3. On stretchable leathers and suede items which receive a lot of stress, such as belts, interface whenever possible.

4. If impossible to interface, always stay-stitch around neck and arm-hole edges.

5. Glue machine-stitched seams open.

6. Glue, rather than sew, hems and waistbands in place.

7. Top-stitch around all edges when sewing soft leathers to prevent stretching and to help flatten seams, neck and armhole edges.

8. Glue applied designs, self belts, etc. even though you will sew them later.

9. Use a very sharp scissors when cutting heavy skins but, if you find this difficult, change to a mat knife or a sharp razor blade.

10. Hammer glued edges lightly with a padded hammer to further flatten folded edges.

11. Coat thread with beeswax by holding the thread against the wax cake with your thumb and drawing it through the wax while twisting it. Pull the thread through several times before sewing. Commercially prepared waxed threads come in different weights.

12. Avoid sharp pointed corners (such as pointed collars), when sewing two layers of leather together, because they don't turn well.

13. Use machine needles for leather or number 11-16 for machine sewing. The needle size will depend on the weight of the leather.

14. Use a long stitch when machine sewing as short stitches may be close enough together to cause the leather to rip.

MAKING FRINGE

1. SELF-FRINGE

Self-fringe is fringe that is cut from the main piece of leather instead of

being added to it. Using a mat knife and steel straightedge, cut the fringe by laying the straightedge along the length of your main piece and cutting it as long or as short as you like. Be sure your fingers press firmly against that part of the steel edge adjacent to the part you're cutting with the mat knife. If this is not done the suede will either slip or pull out from under the ruler and you won't get a straight fringe, or it will stretch as you pull the blade down causing the suede to crimp (cut in wavy lines). Change blades often, because very sharp blades cut straighter and easier (fig. 40).

Fig. 40

2. DOUBLE-HOLE METHOD

For each fringe you must have two holes punched on the main piece. Cut thin, individual strips as long as you want. Point one or both ends and push one end down one hole and up the other. You can add as many as you like, wherever you like, by using this method (fig. 41).

3. SINGLE-HOLE EDGING METHOD

Cut a long strip 3/16-inch wide. Cut a point at both ends. Punch one hole close to the edge to be fringed. Fold the fringe in half with the pointed ends together. Thread these points down through the hole and pull until you have a one-inch loop remaining on the right side. Bring the points around the edge, through the loop and pull tightly (fig. 42). These can also be used as thongs.

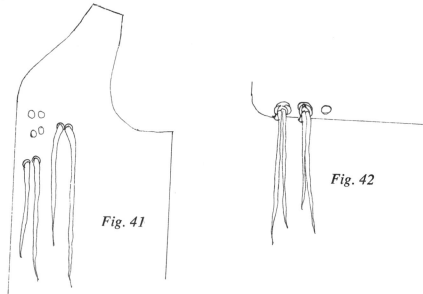

Fig. 41

Fig. 42

4. APPLIED STRIP OF FRINGE

Cut a rectangle of suede or leather as long as you want the fringe, and as wide as the piece you're going to sew it on. Cut the fringe as in method 1, leaving a ½-inch to 1-inch edge uncut at the top. Sew or glue this strip to your otherwise finished garment (fig. 43).

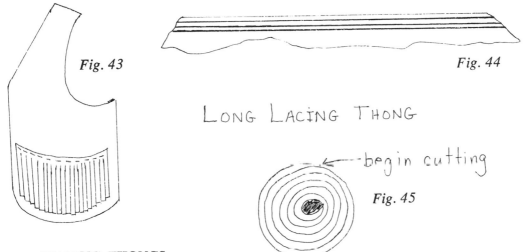

Fig. 43

Fig. 44

LONG LACING THONG

←—begin cutting

Fig. 45

MAKING THONGS

There are three methods for making thongs.

1. Simply cut long thin strips from a straight piece of leather or suede (fig. 44).

2. If very long thongs are needed to lace two pieces of suede together, they can be cut from a circle of suede or soft leather. Start anywhere on the outside edge and cut in one continuous circle, keeping an even distance from the edge at all times until you reach the middle. When you're finished you'll have a curly, thin strip. This would be unsuitable as fringe or as a hanging thong, but is fine for lacing since curves won't show (fig. 45).

3. Tooling cowhide, or stiff leathers can be spliced together to make long thongs. Take two strips to be spliced and bevel one end on each of them by cutting off the excess with a leather knife. To assure bonding apply a strong leather glue to both beveled edges. Weight them (fig. 46) while drying if necessary. Do not use them until they're thoroughly dry.

Thongs are simply long strips used to keep two pieces of leather together, so if you're really creative you could probably find many more ways to achieve the same end. You could knot two shorter strips together to make a longer one or use a strong, thick twine or macrame cord.

Cutting leather into strips either for fringe or thongs can be done in several ways. The use of heavy duty scissors, a mat knife or a leather knife has been demonstrated in this book. Other ways to cut strips are with leather shears, which are scissors with teeth to grip the leather as you cut (fig. 47); a paper cutter or a draw gauge. This last tool consists of a razor attached to one end of a ruler and mounted on a handle. It is adjustable so that it can cut any width desired (fig. 48).

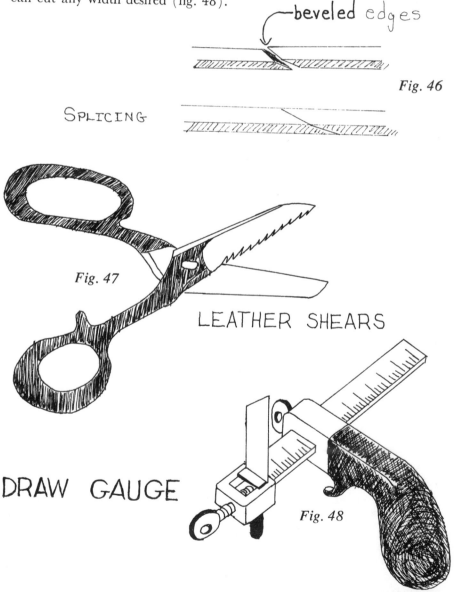

—beveled edges

Fig. 46

SPLICING

Fig. 47

LEATHER SHEARS

DRAW GAUGE

Fig. 48

WORKING WITH THICK LEATHER

There are some techniques that are especially useful when working with thick vegetable-tanned cowhide. These hides have many advantages because they are harder. They can be formed into new shapes by wetting and stretching or bending. They can also be thinned easily, will hold a sharper fold and can be carved and gouged.

BENDING

Play with the leather, bending it in different ways. Try to form it by bending it only into a definite shape. When you have something, skive (thin by shaving) those areas which are going to be permanently attached. Rivets, spots or stitching can be used for this. Wet the leather thoroughly. Bend it into shape. Insert any rivets or spots and let it dry (fig. 49).

FOLDING

Using either a wood-cut gouge, a leather knife or an adjustable leather gouge, which has a device to adjust the depth of the cut (fig. 50) cut a V-shaped groove where it will fold. The groove must be no more than half the depth of the leather (fig. 51). Dampen the leather, holding it in place until it dries. If the leather is to be folded flat, pound it lightly along the fold and weight it down until it dries (fig. 52).

bent leather
tacked to keep
its shape

Fig. 49

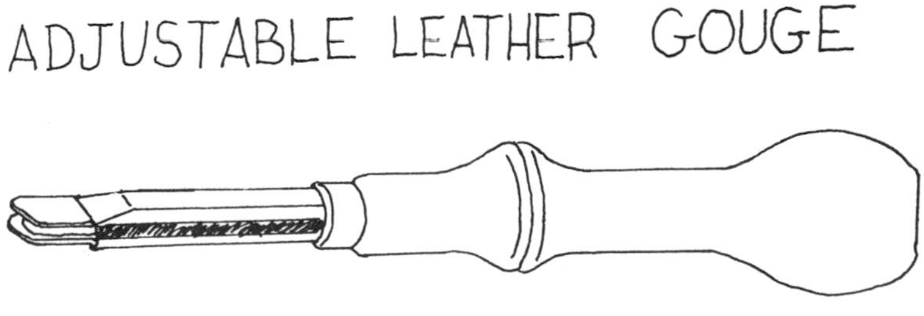

ADJUSTABLE LEATHER GOUGE

Fig. 50

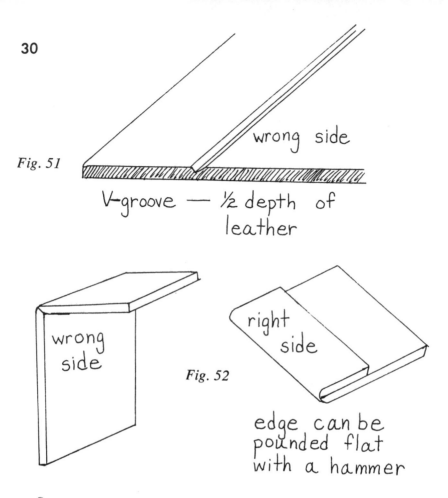

Fig. 51

V-groove — ½ depth of leather

wrong side

wrong side

Fig. 52

right side

edge can be pounded flat with a hammer

SKIVING

When putting two layers of thick leather together, it is often desirable to remove some of the bulk. To do this the pieces are skived or shaved thinner. This process is useful when working on seam edges which will be stitched or laced together as for a purse; when sandwiching layers as for sandal straps and when folding or bending a belt end to double it around a buckle bar.

There are a number of tools that can be used: a leather knife, a head knife (fig. 53), a skiver (fig. 54) or any other sharp tool which you feel comfortable using. Whichever you use, place the edge to be skived on the edge of a workboard so that it's raised. Whenever using sharp tools always cut away from you, never toward your body, and never toward any fingers. Be sure that the fingers holding the leather in place are not in a direct line with the blade but always a safe distance to one side. If the blade does slip, you won't cut yourself. To bevel the edge evenly, apply a steady pressure as you skive.

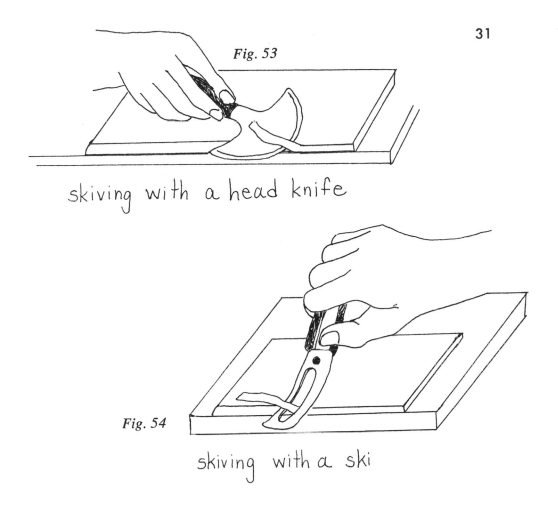

Fig. 53

skiving with a head knife

Fig. 54

skiving with a ski

EDGES

The edges on vegetable-tanned cowhide are likely to fray. Burnishing prevents this from happening. To do this, rub beeswax into the edge with either a hard, rounded metal tool such as a burnisher (fig. 55), a grooved edge slicker (fig. 56) or a combination tool called a bone folder and edge creaser (fig. 57). The procedure in using any of these tools is to rub it back and forth along the edge of the leather, thus setting the wax in the fibers, until a shine appears.

To obtain other edge effects an edge beveler can be used to thin the edges and when burnished can be made round. A line, following the edge of the leather can be made with an edge creaser (fig. 58).

When working with hard, thick leather you'll find a great number of tools available and, if you will get good use from it, very often a special tool is practical. You may also find some of these tools helpful, although not absolutely necessary, when working with softer leathers. How much you wish to invest is up to you. You may not be willing to spend the extra effort and time necessary when working with makeshift tools.

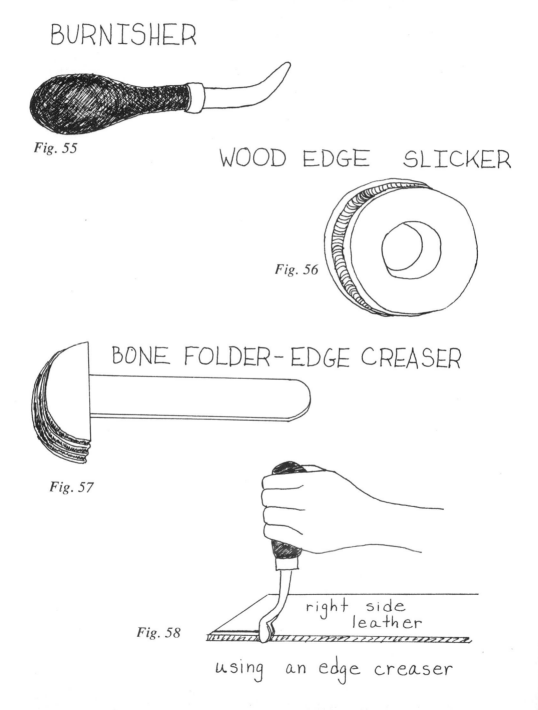

BURNISHER

Fig. 55

WOOD EDGE SLICKER

Fig. 56

BONE FOLDER-EDGE CREASER

Fig. 57

Fig. 58

right side
leather

using an edge creaser

II. Leather picture frame with acrylic paint and decorative nail trim, p. 166.

I. Suede tie-dyed hot pants and midi vest, p. 106.

III. Suede belts: (top left) Glued suede appliqué, p. 76. (top right) Corset with burned design, p. 64. (bottom center) One-piece belt with marking-pen design, p. 57.

IV. (left) Suede hat with embroidered design, p. 120. (right) Book jacket with leather appliqué decoration, p. 170.

VI. Machine sewn vest, p. 96. Suede chokers: (left) Glued appliqué decoration. (center) India ink decoration with marking—pen outline. (right) Marking—pen decoration, p. 54. Leather shoulder bag with acrylic paint design, p. 126.

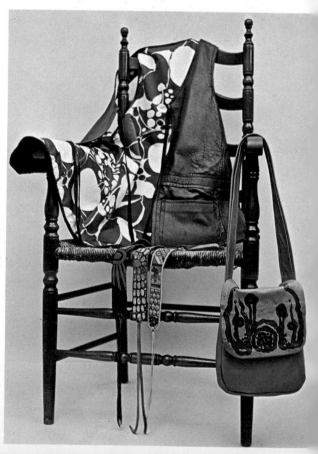

V. (left) Tooled key tab with outline tooling and flat modeling design, it is colored with acrylic paint and leather dye, p. 140. (top right) Incised and stamped bracelet with gold leaf design and leather dye coloring, p. 143. (bottom right) Embossed leather belt buckle colored with India inks, p. 135.

MACHINE SEWING

USING TISSUE PAPER

Tissue paper can be placed on top of, and underneath, leather when machine sewing to protect it from the gripper plate and pressure foot and to help move it through the machine easily. It should be used only when working on the wrong side of leather or on surfaces that will not be seen when the garment is finished. After stitching, the paper is torn away from both sides of the stitching line. When tissue paper is torn away it leaves tiny paper flecks under the stitches which are very difficult to get out.

USING HEAVY BROWN PAPER

When you're sewing on the right side of leather or on areas that will be seen when tne garment is finished, heavy brown paper strips should be used. These strips can be cut from grocery bags. Brown paper is more protective than tissue paper, and even more important, it rips away cleanly, leaving no trace of paper under the stitches. It is necessary to use heavier paper when sewing layers or bulky areas of leather together.

THREADS

WAXED THREAD

Thread is waxed to give it strength. When thread is pulled through leather, the friction caused by the leather rubbing against it very often breaks the thread. You can wax any thread by pulling it over a piece of beeswax repeatedly. Press the thread onto the wax with your thumb. As you pull it through, twist the thread. The heavier your leather the heavier your thread should be. For any leather you should not use anything less than a heavy-duty thread. Various weights of waxed thread are sold in leather supply stores, from 5-ply to 9-ply. The 5-ply is about the thickness of carpet thread and cannot be used when machine sewing. Waxed thread is more difficult to pull through the leather because it has a tendency to catch, but it should be used on any areas where there will be a lot of stress. Even when your item is finished the leather will, in many cases, still be rubbing against that thread and if it isn't waxed it will eventually break.

Carpet Thread

Carpet thread, unwaxed, can be used where strength is needed but where there is less possibility of rubbing later on. Unwaxed thread slips through holes more easily.

Machine Thread

The lightest thread that should be used is heavy-duty mercerized thread, even when working on lightweight leathers or on items where you think no rubbing will occur at all. Leather, being naturally harder and stronger than thread, will eventually break through anything weaker.

Embroidery Threads

Although they can be waxed, they will loose their softness and original character. Since embroidery thread is usually not used for strengthening the construction of the piece, I prefer to use it unwaxed.

STITCHING AND LACING

Stitching

1. Whenever possible start between 2 pieces so that the knotted end of the thread or the end of the laces will not show.
2. To protect stitching that will be subjected to a lot of hard wear, (as in sandals) cut a groove in the top of the leather so that it is half the depth of the leather or less. Stitch in this groove (fig. 59).

Stitches

a. RUNNING STITCH: It *is* just what it sounds like. To do it, push the thread up one hole, down the next, up the next leaving every other space between holes empty (fig. 60).

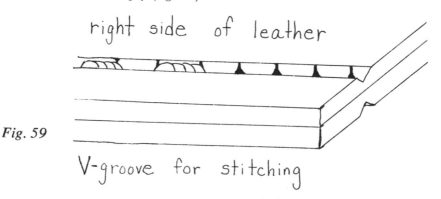

Fig. 59

right side of leather

V-groove for stitching

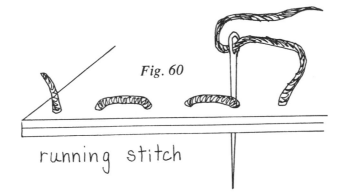

Fig. 60

running stitch

b. BACK STITCH: Push the thread up the first hole, down the second, up the third, back down the second, up the fourth, down the third (fig. 61). This stitich appears as a flat stitch on one side and as a stem or outline stitch on the other.

c. COUCHING STITCH: Two threads must be used. Begin by putting one thread through the first hole and glueing it between the layers. Fasten the other thread between the layers at the same point. Hold the first thread below the line of holes. Bring the second thread over this first thread and insert it back through the same hole. Pull on this second thread until the first thread is pulled partially into the hole (fig. 62). Repeat this for each hole, sewing only with the second thread.

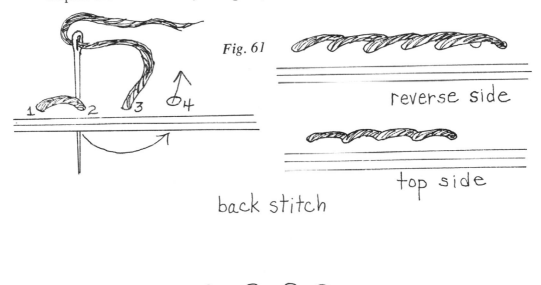

Fig. 61

reverse side

top side

back stitch

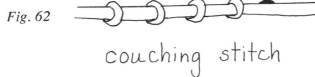

Fig. 62

couching stitch

d. SADDLE STITCH: Using 2 threads on 2 needles knot the end of each thread. Beginning between layers and starting at the same hole go out opposite sides. Both needles will now go through the second hole from opposite sides (fig. 63).

e. LOCKED SADDLE STITCH: Same as the saddle stitch except that before pulling the stitch tight one needle is pulled through the last stitch. This causes the thread to intertwine between the layers or inside the stitching hole (fig. 64).

f. DOUBLE LOCKED SADDLE STITCH: Same as the locked saddle stitch except that both needles are passed through the last stitch before tightening it. This causes the thread to intertwine twice in the stitching hole (fig. 65).

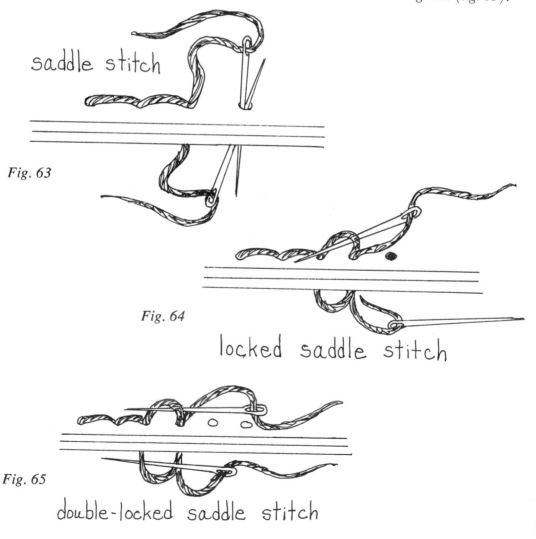

saddle stitch

Fig. 63

Fig. 64

locked saddle stitch

Fig. 65

double-locked saddle stitch

LACING

Laces can be bought as well as hand-made. They can be purchased flat or round in a variety of colors and in leather or plastic.

    1. Lacing is never started on a corner.

    2. Laces should be tightened every 10 stitches or so. To do this insert the awl under each lace and pull taut.

    3. To see if your lacing is tight enough try pushing them from side to side. You should not be able to do this. However, they should not be tight enough as to cause the edge to pucker.

    4. For a nice finishing touch you can lightly hammer the edges flat.

    5. Unless otherwise specified, all holes should be placed about ¼-inch from the edge of the leather.

    a. WHIP STITCH: The lace must be 3 times as long as the distance to be laced and as wide as the holes will take. Most lacing should not be more than ¼-inch wide. Begin between layers by gluing the lace end down. Lace out the first hole, loop it over the edge of the leather and through the second hole from the back (fig. 66). Lace twice through each corner hole. Lace through the last single hole so that you are between layers again, and glue this edge down.

    b. CROSS LACING: For this lacing you must punch an even number of holes. Cut two laces and begin them at the same point between layers. Push them out through opposite sides. Bring the lace on the wrong side over the edges to the front and put it through the second hole (fig. 67). Loop the other lace over the edges to the wrong side and push it through the third hole to the front (fig. 68). Continue in this manner using one lace, then the other. To make neat lacing, do not change the order in which you lace them. At the corners put two stitches in each corner hole.

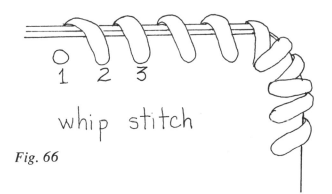

whip stitch

Fig. 66

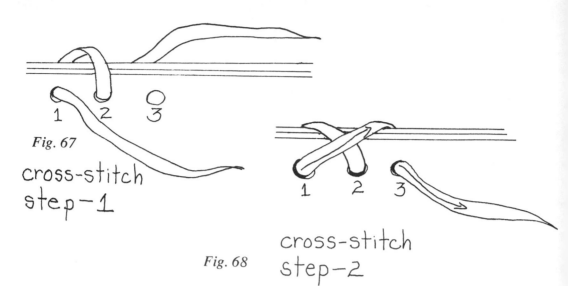

Fig. 67

cross-stitch
step—1

Fig. 68

cross-stitch
step—2

c. BUTTONHOLE LACING: Because this is a rather bulky stitch, use as thin
a lace as possible, or space your holes further apart than usual. You'll
need a lace 6 times the distance to be laced. Begin on the side facing
you and pass the lace to the wrong side leaving a good 2-inches loose
on the right side (fig. 69). Bring the lace around the front of this lace
and pass it through the second hole from the right to the wrong side
(fig. 70). Bring the lace over the edges to the right side again and pass
it under the lace that is through the second hole (fig. 71). Continue
lacing. At the corner holes, lace two stitches through each hole (fig.
72). Lace around to your starting point. Remove the lacing from the
first and second hole (fig. 73). Put the lace you just removed through
the second hole from the wrong side and between the layers. Lace as
usual through hole 1 (fig. 74). To end the lacing put the end through
the open loop, down through hole 2, ending between the layers (fig.
75).

d. FLORENTINE LACING: This is done with soft leather. You need laces
about 3 times the distance to be laced. Laces should be about ⅜-inches
wide. The distance between the holes must be the same as the lace
width and the same distance from the edge of the leather. Lacing is
the same procedure as for the whip stitch, with the exception that 3
stitches should be in the corner hole (fig. 76).

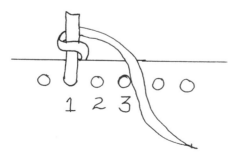

buttonhole stitch
step — 1

Fig. 69

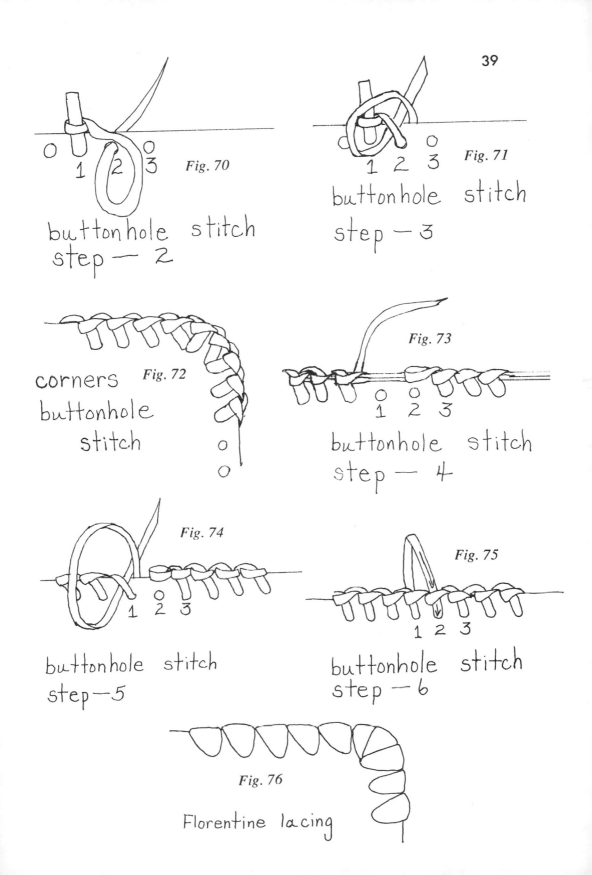

Fig. 70

buttonhole stitch
step — 2

Fig. 71

buttonhole stitch
step — 3

corners
buttonhole
stitch

Fig. 72

Fig. 73

buttonhole stitch
step — 4

Fig. 74

buttonhole stitch
step—5

Fig. 75

buttonhole stitch
step — 6

Fig. 76

Florentine lacing

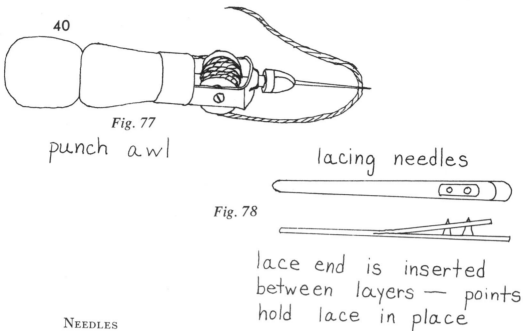

40

Fig. 77

punch awl

lacing needles

Fig. 78

lace end is inserted
between layers — points
hold lace in place

NEEDLES

When stitching or lacing there are a number of needles you can use. You can use a punch type stitching awl (fig. 77) which is the most automatic of the devices available; glover's needles (see section on tools); harness needles (see section on tools) or lacing needles (fig. 78).

MAKING HOLES FOR STITCHING

Among those tools available for making holes for stitching are the revolving punch (see section on tools). This tool can be purchased with a number of attachments including a slit prong chisel. Stitching chisels can be flat multiple-pronged (see tool section) to create a slit cut, they can be round (fig. 79) for round holes or they can be either round or flat single-pronged drive punches (fig. 80). You can make holes with an awl (see tool section(or any other sharp object that you find suitable including a hand drill.

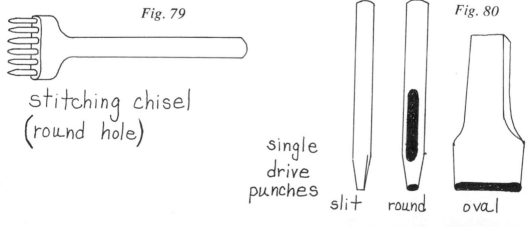

Fig. 79

Fig. 80

stitching chisel
(round hole)

single
drive
punches   slit   round   oval

OTHER HELPFUL TOOLS WHEN STITCHING

Other tools you might find useful are a pair of pliers to help pull the needle or lace through the leather when it becomes very difficult. To help keep the stitching an even distance from the edge of the leather you might use an edge creaser (see fig. 58), a stitch spacer (fig. 81), or any other tool that can make an indentation, including a ruler and a knitting needle. All these tools mark the leather edge in some way. To hold the leather firmly in place (especially useful with heavy leathers) you can use a professional stitching pony (fig. 82), a smaller stitching pony (fig. 83), a homemade stitching pony (fig. 84) made with 2 pieces of wood and a C-clamp, or simply hold the leather very tightly between your knees while stitching.

Fig. 81

stitch spacer

bench stitching pony
Fig. 82

Fig. 83

stitching pony

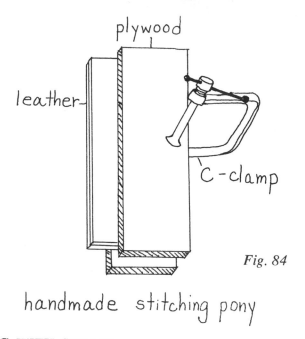

plywood

leather

C-clamp

Fig. 84

handmade stitching pony

WORKING WITH SCRAPS

There are many different things to do with scraps and using them is easy if you keep in mind that a project doesn't necessarily have to be cut from one piece. The designs for the sectioned belts in the beginning of this book originated because I didn't have enough suede to make a belt in one piece. Usually, I buy skins for a vest or skirt and then put the remaining scraps together to make a smaller article. The leftover pieces from these scraps are then used for appliqués.

DESIGNS AND DECORATIONS

Adapting a design is simply the process of changing one form of presentation into another to suit the size, texture and materials you're working with. To do this, sometimes a great deal of distortion of the original design is necessary and even desirable. We adapt many different things that we come in contact with in many areas of our lives without realizing it. Adapting something we see to create a design only seems difficult because it's not something we do all the time. With practice this process will come as easily as dusting with a paper towel when a dust cloth is not available.

When an artist creates a work of art which includes elements from someone else's work, but to which he adds new elements, he's creating something unique. He is really not copying; he is using his ingenuity to combine old elements into a new form. All artists "borrow" from other artists. In other fields of endeavor this process is sometimes called progress.

All you need, to begin adapting designs, is to open your eyes and start looking around you. There are design possibilities in everything—an orange, a cut-open tomato, the wood grain on your floor, petals, stones.

Artists and craftsmen are always looking for fresh or new ideas and strangely enough they often refer to old artifacts and art work to do this. You might start by looking through a magazine. Look closely at the illustrations, photos and color combinations. When you see something that pleases you, make a small rough sketch of it. You may use a shape from one photo and a line from another or even parts of an illustration that has appeal. Draw a rough sketch combining all the areas you chose. Try rearranging these shapes, changing their sizes or spreading them out. Do not try to draw objects realistically, instead simplify them. If you wish, you can always try to make them more realistic later.

Whether your design is simple or intricate, abstract or realistic, will be dictated largely by the materials you choose to work with. For instance, simple forms lend themselves best to glued appliqué. However, when using acrylic paints you can be as realistic as you like.

Once you have 5 or 6 sketches, consider the piece you're going to decorate. If the sketch you like best, fills a square area, and you want to use it on a long rectangular belt, consider the possibility of repeating it a few times around the belt. If it is fairly complicated, consider separating its parts and spreading them out around the belt. Working with what you have, consider other shapes that would help fill in the design, consider variations of the same form, or perhaps use another media such as paints, inks, etc. to make it more interesting.

Drawing Shapes

CIRCLES: If a small circle is needed, trace the bottom of a coffee can, glass, or ink bottle, or use a compass.

Larger circles are more difficult. You must first find the center of the paper or cloth.

1. To do this rule diagonal lines from each set of opposite corners. The point at which they intersect, is the center (fig. 85).

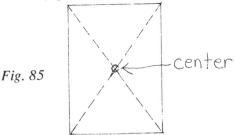

Fig. 85

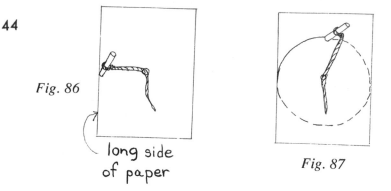

Fig. 86

long side
of paper

Fig. 87

2. Tie a length of string to a piece of chalk, a pen or a pencil. Place the chalk at the outer edge of the long side of the paper and run the string tightly to the center mark (fig. 86).

3. Holding the string firmly on the center mark, swing the chalk around to make one full circle (fig. 87).

OVALS: 1. Draw a straight line in the middle of the paper a little longer than your oval will be. Mark the center of the line with pen or pencil and letter it as point A. Placing a compass on this point, swing tiny arcs to cross both ends of this line. Mark as points B and C. This indicates the length of the oval (fig. 88).

2. Draw line D-E through point A to cross line B-C at a 90° angle (fig. 89).

3. Lay a straight paper strip, slightly longer than the distance from point A to C. Mark these points on the strip with arrows and number them 1 and 2. At the same time mark the exact center between these two points with an arrow and designate this as point 3 on the paper strip (fig. 90).

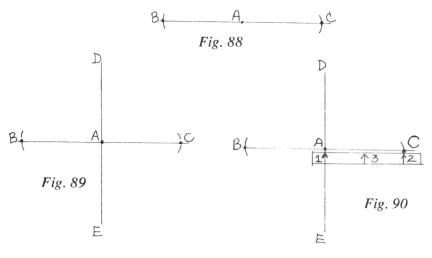

Fig. 88

Fig. 89

Fig. 90

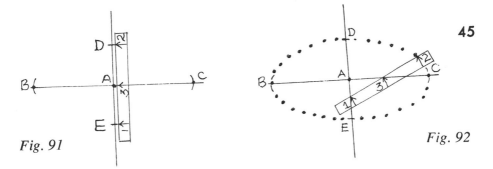

Fig. 91

Fig. 92

4. Place this strip along line D-E placing point 3 at point A. Make marks on line D-E at points 1 and 2 (fig. 91).

5. Move point 3 along line A-C while simultaneously moving point 1 along line A-E. Each time you move the strip make a dot opposite point 2. Continue rotating the paper clockwise until you have many dots in one quarter of the intersecting lines. Connect these dots (fig. 92).

6. Repeat this procedure in the 3 remaining quarters.

STARS: 1. Draw a circle, using a compass or the method previously described. Use a measuring tape to measure the perimeter of the circle. Divide this measurement into 5 equal parts. Use this measurement to mark 5 equidistant points around the circle. Mark as points A (fig. 93). Connect these points with straight lines to form a pentagon.

2. Using the center of the original circle draw an inner circle about halfway inside it, with a compass. Draw dotted lines from all points marked A through the center of the circle, to bisect the pentagon side opposite it (fig. 94). Designate these as lines B. Where dotted lines cross inner circle, mark point C.

3. Draw lines from points A to points C all around. This will form the star (fig. 95).

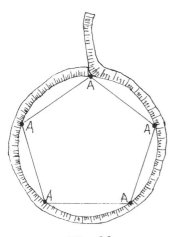

Fig. 93

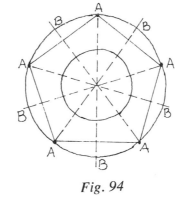

Fig. 94

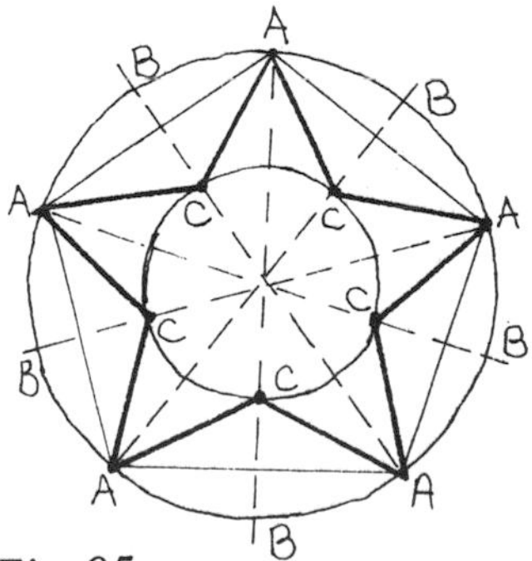

Fig. 95

ENLARGING AND REDUCING DESIGNS

1. Mark off squares on your design or on a tracing of your design. The squares can be ⅛-inch, ¼-inch, ½-inch, etc. depending upon the size of the design.

2. If you want to enlarge the design to 6 times its present size your second piece of paper must be 6 times as large as your original. Once you have determined how many times you want to enlarge, cut your paper to this size.

3. Mark the same number of squares onto this paper as there are on the original design, enlarging each square as many times as you enlarged the paper itself. If, for instance, each square on your small original design was ¼ inch, and you're enlarging 6 times, each square on your larger sheet will be 1½ inches (fig. 96).

4. You now copy, as accurately as possible, the design from each smaller square into each corresponding larger square (fig. 97).

Reverse this process for reducing a design.

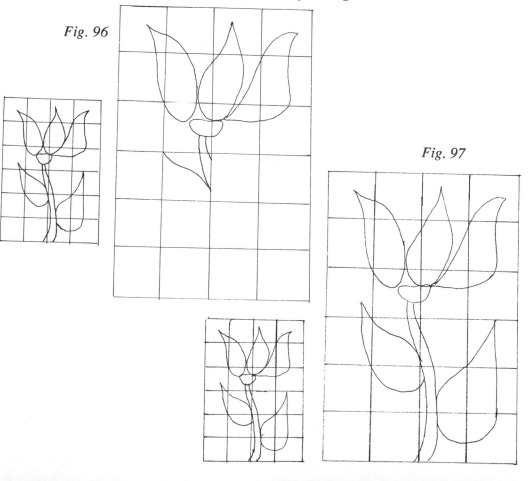

Fig. 96

Fig. 97

STENCILING

Stenciling is useful when you want to repeat a design exactly. This is also the best way to mass-produce an item.

In preparing a design to be stenciled, remember that you must leave spaces between shapes if you want them to be legible when printed. Each shape you draw will be cut out (fig. 98). If all the shapes are touching or overlapping, when you cut them out you'll have one big hole in your stencil paper. Stencil paper is preferred because it is specially treated to resist liquids. If it were not, it would fall apart with repeated use.

Draw your design on ordinary paper, to the exact measurements of the piece you'll be working on. Place the stencil paper over this drawing and trace, using a pencil and pressing lightly. If you dig into the stencil paper, the edges of your stenciled design will be fuzzy. Tape both pieces down to keep them from slipping.

Use an X-acto blade or mat knife to cut around the shapes. When cutting, place cardboard underneath to protect the work surface. Hold the blade at an angle toward the cutout shape to create a beveled edge (fig. 99). This will keep the paint from creeping under the paper. Cut all the way through the paper the first time, to keep the edges smooth.

Using commercially prepared stencil paints will assure you of clean outlines, if the manufacturer's directions are followed. Acrylics can be used straight from the tube. Any paint you use must be thick and paste-like. If watery paint is used it will get under the edges and blot.

Put newspaper under the item to be stenciled, to be safe. Lay the stencil in place on the item. Both pieces can be taped down or held firmly in place with your hand. Apply paint with a brush which has very little paint on it (almost dry) by brushing into the open areas. Always work from the edge of the opening into the center (fig. 100). If the area is not completely covered by paint the first time, repeat the process. Never hurry the stenciling by loading your brush.

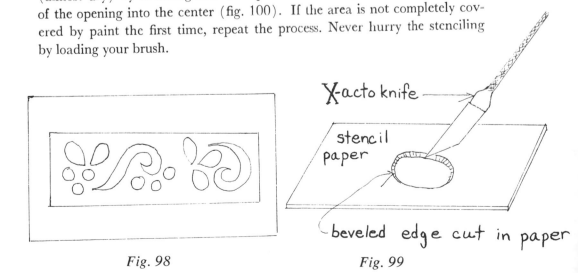

Fig. 98   Fig. 99

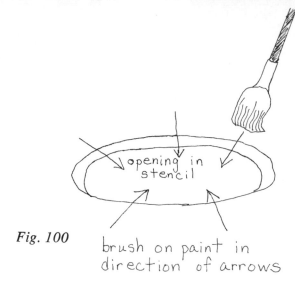

Fig. 100 brush on paint in direction of arrows

To shade one of these areas, simply darken a portion of it by applying more paint of the same color or cut another stencil for these areas.

Don't wash the stencil. To clean, turn it on the wrong side, and using a little cleaning fluid on a soft cloth, gently rub the paint off. Vigorous rubbing may tear it.

LEATHER DYES, FINISHES AND PAINTS

DYES

Dyes and finishes can be applied to almost any leather. Dyes add color. Finishes protect, soften or condition the otherwise finished piece.

Follow the instructions for applying dyes as given by the manufacturer. Dyes, paints, inks or any coloring may be applied with brushes, daubers, sponges, pens, cotton, padded felt or cloth, Q-tips, pipe cleaners or paper towels.

LIQUID LEATHER DYES: Liquid dyes penetrate the leather deeply and quickly and have a dull sheen which can usually be polished to a soft luster. They come in a wide variety of colors and can be mixed to make additional colors. When applied to wet leather, color becomes dark because pores are open. When applied to dry leather, lighter tones result because pores are closed.

ANTIQUE DYES: Antique dyes which come in a paste form take a few minutes (as compared to liquid dyes which take a few seconds), to stain the leather, and they do not penetrate as deeply. They are most effective when used on tooled leather because the paste is caught in the depressions, creating darker areas, and wiped off the top surfaces leaving it lighter in color. When used on plain leather it brings out beautiful subtleties in the grain. It can be polished to a high luster to create a rich patina. Antique dyes are not waterproof and should therefore be finished with a wax coating or leather lacquer. When applying lacquer the dye should first be set with a resin primer to prevent bleeding and to prevent the lacquer from flaking.

EDGE DYES: Edge dyes are used not only to color edges but also to smooth the edge fibers and keep them from fraying. It dries to a low luster and penetrates quickly.

EDGE ENAMELS: Edge enamels serve the same purpose as edge dyes but are not as penetrating or as permanent as edge dyes. They dry glossy without polishing.

EDGE INKS: Edge inks, because they are wax based, must be set with a warm edging tool. They penetrate thoroughly and result in an opaque, glossy edge.

Edge-Kote is a water repellent product which dries to a soft luster.

Always test dyes on scrap leather before applying. Keep in mind that the same piece of leather will often not dye evenly due to natural imperfections in the piece. Usually this effect is pleasant. Drastic differences are usually due to something you have done wrong in either preparing the leather or applying the dyes. Leather must be cased and any artificial finish removed before applying dyes.

All of the dyes listed come in a great variety of colors.

FINISHES

After dyeing, a protective finish should be applied.

LEATHER LACQUER: Leather lacquer is probably the strongest protective finish for leather. It will not discolor the underfinish and will keep dyes from fading. It may be brushed, wiped or sprayed on, and can be thinned with lacquer thinner. Usually a lacquer primer must be applied first, making the use of this type of finish a two-step process.

WAX FINISHES: Wax finishes come in liquid, cake and stick form. The liquid will result in a soft velvety luster. Stick wax is usually applied by a machine and results in a high luster, but if it has been softened by warming, it can be applied by hand. It results in a soil-resistant finish. Burnishing wax comes in a cake form and is used to produce a high edge gloss. Carnauba wax is also in cake form and results in a soft luster coating.

RESIN: Resin finishes will alter the underlying color, resulting in a mellow gloss. Although not as durable as lacquer it is easier to apply and results in a soft, satiny appearance.

OTHER FINISHES: Neat's-foot Compound Oil (see Sources) is used to waterproof as well as soften leather. It will darken natural leather slightly and if applied and put in strong sunlight will often darken it drastically.

Saddle soap may be used to clean, soften and condition leathers. It comes in paste form.

Lexol will restore natural oils to leather and comes in liquid form. It mellows natural colored leather.

Leather balm is used on smooth leathers to clean, preserve, polish and restore them. It also inhibits surface stains.

Silicone paste wax is water repellent. It produces a high gloss and comes in earthy colors.

Acrylic polymer mediums and varnish can be used over acrylic and enamel paints and over some dyes. The final finish can be made to vary from mat to a high gloss.

Before applying a finish to your completed piece it would be wise to experiment on a scrap of the same leather first to be sure that it will not damage your particular undercoating and to be sure that you will get the effect you want.

TEXTILE DYES

Textile dyes are meant to be used on fabric, therefore, when used on a material as hard as leather, they do not penetrate as completely as leather dyes, resulting in a light, or wash effect. When applied to suedes the results are less predictable; it may turn very dark, or it may turn colorless, making the suede look as though it has wet spots. That's why I suggest experimenting with a scrap first.

Liquid textile dyes can be handled in a number of ways. Use 3 to 5 tablespoons of dye to 1 or 2 inches of water in a 12 x 18-inch pan to produce normal shades. If you want a lighter shade, add more water; for a darker shade, add more dye. The water should be hot, but never boiling. A small amount of liquid dishwashing detergent will help set the color in materials like suede, which are resistant to these dyes.

1. They can be used for tie-dyeing light colored cow-split suede. On darker cow-splits the colors will be muted and sometimes change entirely. When using dark-colored hides experiment first.

2. They can be painted on tooling or chrome-tanned cowhide and often look like washes (light tints of colors). They can be darkened by applying the same color to the same area repeatedly and can be lightened by diluting them with cold water. Experiment with scraps before applying them to dry or damp leather.

3. They can be dripped, poured or swirled onto split suede cowhide which is tacked and stretched on a ceiling tile or large board. If different colors are used at the same time they will mix and produce unusual shades and hues.

Dry dyes can be used in the same way but first you must mix a concentrated solution according to package directions.

BLEACH

Make a diluted solution of half bleach and half water and apply it to those areas you want lightened. Follow this with an application of straight bleach. When the areas you're bleaching begin to fuzz, wash the suede thoroughly in cool water to remove the bleach. No matter how weak your bleach solution is, bleaching does weaken the fibers and if you're not careful, might burn through the piece completely.

Try tie-dyeing using bleach. This will remove the color from those areas not tied together. Be sure to rinse the leather *thoroughly*.

INDIA INKS

1. India inks can be purchased in a wide variety of colors.

2. Because the color of the leather or suede will change the ink colors it is important to experiment with them on a scrap before working on your finished piece.

3. Suede is very absorbent so the ink colors (like textile dyes) tend to appear to be colorless, dark spots.

4. To get cleaner, brighter colors, apply them over white ink; sometimes they even look fluorescent.

5. Interesting colors can be mixed; try mixing them over a coat of white as well as by themselves.

ACRYLICS

Acrylic paints have many advantages over other paints. They are mixed with water, dry quickly, bond firmly to any surface, are waterproof, and are generally more brilliant.

1. Mix paint with water to use.
2. Use gel medium to keep paints moist for a long time.
3. To obtain transparent glazes mix polymer medium with the paint.
   a. Using a glossy polymer medium will result in a shiny glaze; a semi-gloss or semi-mat will result in a low luster; a mat medium will result in a dull or flat finish.
   b. The more polymer medium you use the more transparent the glaze becomes.
   c. One glaze can be used over another, or over a solid color to obtain a new color (i.e. yellow over red produces an orange). Always put the lighter color over the darker one.
   d. Polymer mediums can often be used as a glue but be sure it states this on the bottle.
   e. Polymer mediums can also be used as a final coat to protect the surface of an object. When used on leather it will darken the color.
4. Acrylics come in a wide variety of colors or you can mix your own by using the 3 primary colors—yellow (cadmium yellow light), red (cadmium red medium), blue (permanent or Prussian blue) and black and white. Black will darken your colors (i.e. added to green it produces an olive). White will produce milky or light colors (i.e. red and yellow plus white will produce milky orange, red plus white will produce pink).
5. Since they dry quickly, paint dripped on clothing or mistakes must be wiped off with a damp sponge or wet paper towel immediately; keep a can of water handy.
6. For the same reason, clean brushes immediately after use. As a final wash for brushes use soap and water.

OIL PAINTS

1. Paint directly on leather or spray the leather first with a plastic spray or use a polymer medium to seal it. Sealing will prevent the oils from penetrating the leather thus keeping the colors brilliant.
2. Thin your oil paints with linseed oil or turpentine.
3. Use turpentine to clean brushes and tools.

4. When the oils have dried, apply a second coat of spray or polymer medium to keep the paint from flaking.

Batik (Wax-Resist)

1. Melt paraffin or beeswax in the top of a double boiler. If wax is melted directly over heat it may ignite.

2. Brush the melted wax on the leather wherever you don't want color.

3. To dye the leather, use leather or textile dyes or specially prepared batik dyes.

4. When dry, place newspaper over the waxed areas and press the paper with a hot iron. The wax will melt and the newspaper will absorb it. Use fresh pieces of newspaper until all the wax is absorbed.

5. For a second color, brush wax on other areas of the leather. Wherever the first color is not covered by wax, a third color will be created by the mixing or overlapping of the first and second color (fig. 101). When batiking with more than one color and especially when overlapping to create other colors you should plan the piece carefully and experiment first to be sure not only that you'll get the desired effect but that the leather you're working with is suitable for batik.

6. Another effect can be created by cracking the wax so that the coloring penetrates these cracks. To do this crush the leather after the wax has been applied.

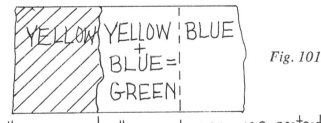

Fig. 101

yellow area protected by wax — remains yellow | yellow area without wax —when blue is added area turns green | area was protected by wax when yellow was applied — wax removed before blue was applied

3. Leather Fashions

SUEDE CHOKER

We begin by making a simple choker. This project will give you the basic technique for measuring items with exactness.

MATERIALS

Split suede cowhide or a suede scrap 5 x 11 inches
Wiss #29 or other heavy duty scissors
Revolving spring hole punch
Ruler
½-yard heavyweight Pellon (optional, see note)
Leather glue (used here: Du-All Super #88)
Ball-point pen or a piece of chalk.

MARKING OFF A RECTANGLE

Select your suede and examine both sides carefully. The clearest, least marked side is the right side. Choose a work area that is large enough to accommodate the entire piece and spread it out. Turn the piece over with the wrong side facing up. This is the side you should always work on; if your pen slips you won't spoil the side that will show. Place your ruler along one edge of the suede. With the pen, mark off 11-inches. Now place your ruler at a right angle to this line; measure down 1¼-inches; make a mark. Place your ruler further along this 11-inch line and mark off 1¼-inches again. Using these marks as a guideline, draw another 11-inch line parallel to the first 11-inch line (plate 1). Join both ends with pen marks, making a rectangle 11 x 1¼-inches (fig. 102). Cut out this shape along the pen lines. You can round off the sides (fig. 103) or scallop the edges for a more decorative effect (fig. 104).

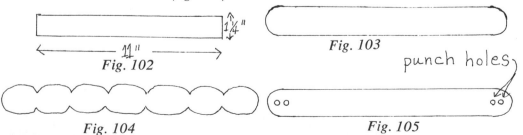

1¼"

Fig. 103

11"

Fig. 102

punch holes

Fig. 104

o o

o o

Fig. 105

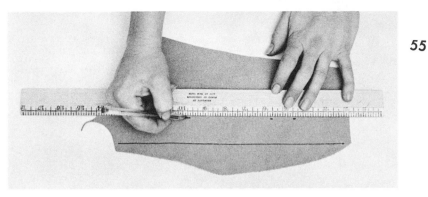

Plate 1

Plate 2   *Plate 3*

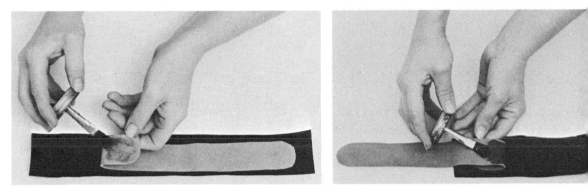

Backing With Pellon

Cut a piece of Pellon ¼-inch larger all around than your suede choker. Place the choker on top of the Pellon, right side up. This will help you line them up properly before gluing them together. Leaving the suede and Pellon flat on the table, lift one end of the choker, being careful to keep both pieces in position. Apply glue, a few inches at a time, to the wrong side of the leather (plate 2). Press the suede onto the Pellon with your fingers. Be careful that you don't get glue on your hand and thus onto the suede. Lift up the other end of the suede as far as it will go without lifting off the portion you have already glued (plate 3). Continuing from the glued portion, apply glue a few inches at a time until the entire piece is glued to the Pellon. Be sure to press the suede firmly as you go, or the two pieces may not bond together properly.

Adding Thongs

When the glue has dried, trim the excess Pellon around the edges. Using the third largest hole on your revolving punch, punch 2 holes in each end (fig. 105). From your leftover scrap, cut 2 strips, called thongs, approxi-

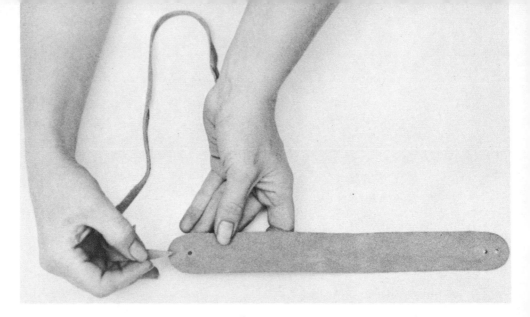

Plate 4

mately ¼-inch wide by 11-inches long. Knot each thong at one end only. Pull the knot as tight as you can and keep it as close to the end as possible. Cut the other end of each thong at an angle to form a point (plate 4). Thread this pointed end down through one hole and up through the other so that both the knot and the loose end can be seen on the outside of your choker. Cut the excess end off each knot. Now tie it around your neck (plate 5).

Note: Pellon is an optional item. It is used to give added body to the piece, prevent stretching, and avoid wear and tear from sweat. Buy black for dark items, and white for the lighter shades.

Plate 5

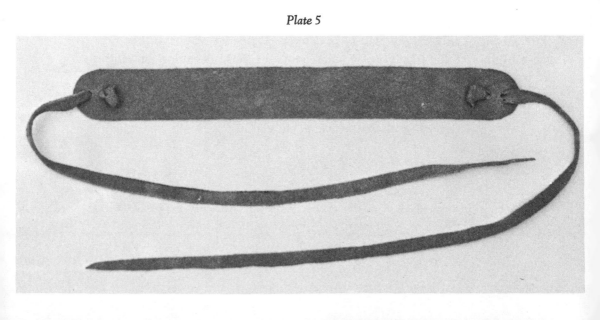

ONE-PIECE LEATHER BELT

The most important feature of this project is the decoration, rather than the belt itself. Choose a pliable leather, because one end of the belt will be flipped over the other in front. When you buy your leather you'll find many different thicknesses. (The thicker the leather, the stiffer it is.) Also, look for a leather with a dull finish that will absorb the marking pen colors. A shiny finish will resist the color so that it will rub off.

MATERIALS

> Pliable leather skin, 4 feet x 6 inches, with a dull finish (used here: 4 or 5-ounce split cowhide)
> Yardstick
> Nylon and felt tip marking pens, one black and others in your choice of colors
> Scissors
> Revolving punch
> Pen or chalk

TESTING MARKER COLORS

Choose a light to medium color leather if you want a bold effect. Marking pens used on darker leathers result in a subtle contrast. Many ink colors have a tendency to change on the leather, and some inks may not show up at all on dark skins. Test colors on a scrap piece first. When they dry you'll see how they're going to look on your finished belt (plate 6).

Check your piece for flaws on both sides. Cuts, holes, scars, and blemishes may occur in an awkward place, spoiling your design, therefore, choose as flawless a piece as possible . . . you may not be able to cut around the flaw.

Using the same measuring techniques as you did for the choker, mark off lines, with your yardstick, at least 20-inches longer than your waist size and 2½-inches wide.

Cut out the piece. Rounding off the ends of your belt will give it a more professional and finished look (fig. 106).

Fig. 106

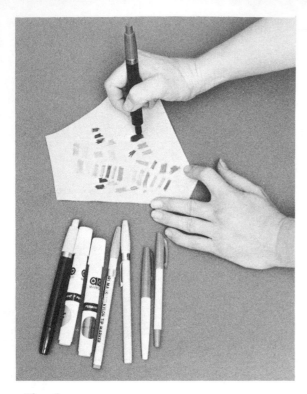

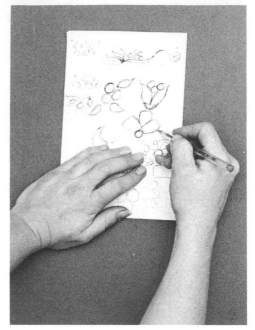

Plate 7

Plate 6

Collecting Ideas

Decorating your belt is perhaps the hardest part of this project. There are several ways you can approach this problem. Ideas do not simply pop out of thin air. We are all influenced by everything we see. I'm constantly looking through magazines and newspapers for designs that catch my eye. Sometimes it's a wallpaper ad, a design on a dress in a clothing ad, a toy, or even a rug. I also look through art books, craft books or for that matter any book with pictures in it. At other times, I get ideas from flowers, trees and insects.

Although it's preferable that you evolve, or at least adapt, a design you see to make it your own, copying is not necessarily a bad thing and can be a good starting place for beginners.

Drawing Freehand

Drawing your design freehand is a much simpler process than most people think; it will add character and individuality to your work. If you're not very confident about your drawing ability, you might practice sketching simple shapes on a piece of paper until you find a few you like (plate 7). After awhile, you'll find drawing is really not so difficult.

If this method doesn't appeal to you, you might make a paper pattern of the belt. Then you can fool around with your design on the paper pattern before you put it on the leather. This can be done as many times as you like, until you're satisfied with the effect.

Now that you've decided on your own design (or on using mine) outline the design on the belt with your black marking pen (plate 8). Fill in the areas made by the outline with your other colored markers (plate 9).

Plate 8

Plate 9

ONE-PIECE SUEDE BELT

MATERIALS

        Split suede cowhide
        Pellon
        Scissors
        Leather glue (used here: Du-All Super #88)
        Revolving punch
        Assorted felt and nylon tip marking pens
        Steel straightedge or yardstick

Taking the same precautions as in the previous projects (to work on the wrong side of your suede), mark your waist size onto it. This time, though, make your second parallel line 5-inches from the first (fig. 107).

Cut a Pellon backing ¼-inch larger all around. This excess allows for stretching and assures that you will not be left with the suede piece larger than the Pellon. Glue the suede to the Pellon. When dry, cut off the excess Pellon and round the corners.

Apply your design with marking pens the same way you did on the leather belt (plate 10). Test your colors on a scrap first. You'll find the colors change even more on suede than they do on leather.

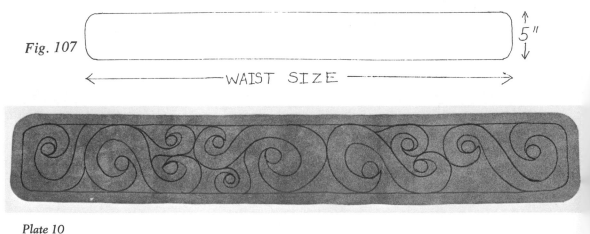

Fig. 107

Plate 10

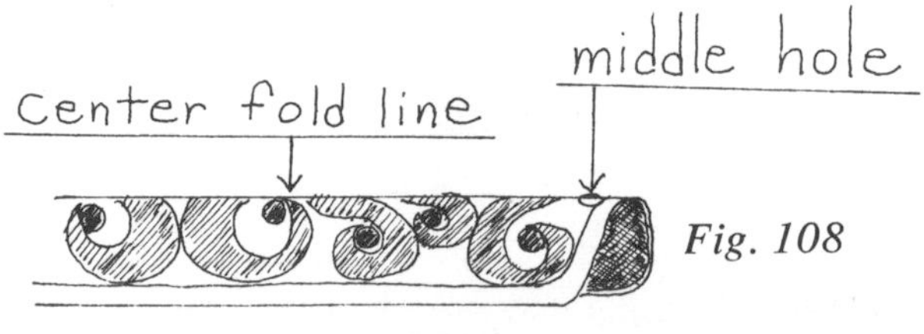

Fig. 108

SPACING HOLES EVENLY

Using the second largest hole on your revolving punch, make three holes on each front end of your belt (plate 11). To line these holes up properly, fold the belt in half the long way, right side out. Punch a hole where the belt folds, about ½-inch in from the edge (fig. 108). Make 2 more holes on each side of this one, about 1½-inches apart. Now fold the belt in half the wide way, matching the edges. With right sides together, mark through these holes with a pen (plate 12). Punch through the pen marks.

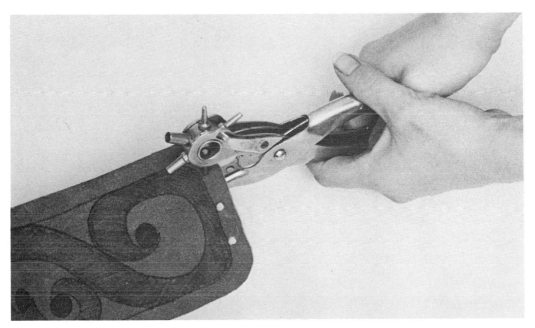

Plate 11

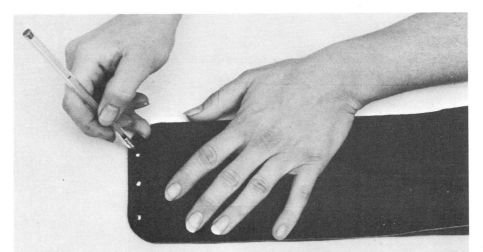

Plate 12

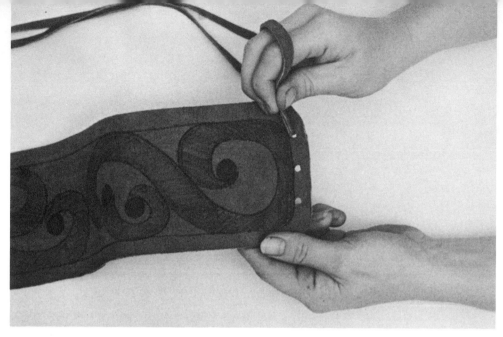

Plate 13

Single Hole Thongs

Cut 10 thongs from the remaining scraps, each 32-inches long. Clip both ends of all thongs to a point. Fold each thong in half so that you have both points between your fingers. Push these points through one of the holes on the right side (plate 13). Pull the doubled thong through the hole until you have a ½-inch loop left on the right side (plate 14). Bring the points up around the edge of the belt and pass them through the loop (plate 15). Pull tighter until there is hardly any slack left (plate 16).

To finish the belt, lace all thongs through the holes in this way (plate 17).

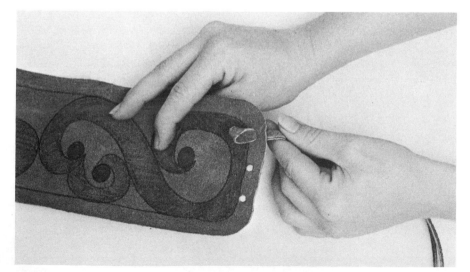

Plate 14

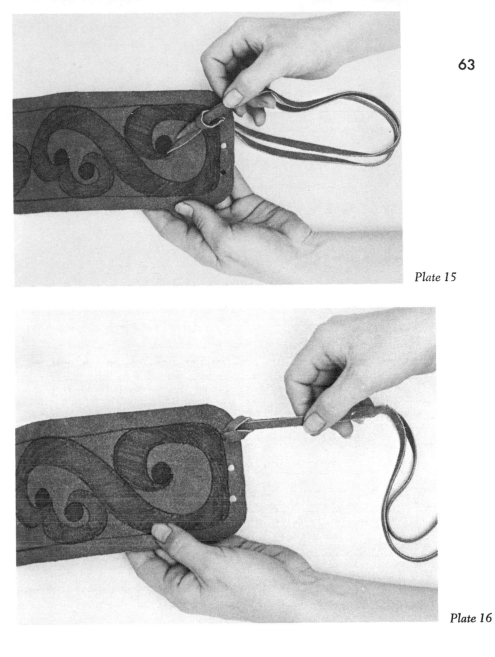

Plate 15

Plate 16

Plate 17

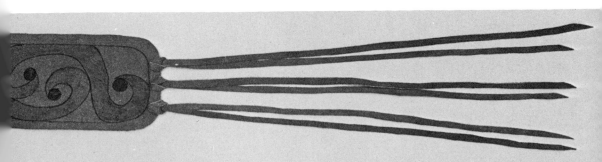

SUEDE CORSET BELT

Materials

    Split suede cowhide in light color (used here: orange-gold)
    Pellon
    Soldering iron
    Piece of asbestos or cork
    10 bound hooks
    Steel straightedge or yardstick
    Scissors
    Leather glue (used here: Du-All Super #88)

Using the same techniques for measuring as in the preceding projects, mark off your waist size plus 2-inches. These extra inches will be needed for the belt to fit around your rib cage. Make your second parallel line 7-inches from the first (fig. 109). Some people may find this width uncomfortable. I suggest you try it on before going further and if necessary trim it down.

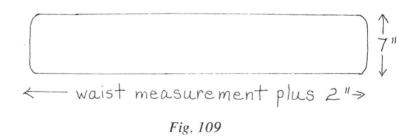

Fig. 109

Burning A Design

Let the soldering iron heat for awhile before trying to use it. It must get very hot. Let it rest on the asbestos or piece of cork to keep your working surface from getting burned.

    You might want to experiment by using the iron on a scrap piece of suede. Try using the flat side for broad marks and the thin edge for finer lines. Twisting it around on one of its corners will create dots (plate 18, 19 and figs. 110-112).

VII. Suede hat with embroidered design, p. 120. Pillow with leather appliqué owl and embroidery, p. 173. Fringed vest (variation of the one on p. 88) with India ink design.

VIII. Fringed vest with beads, p. 88.

IX. Table covering of felt with glued suede appliqués, p. 178.

X. Back view of suede jacket with machine appliqué decoration, p. 116.

XI. Woven wall hanging using suede and leather strips, p. 211.

XII. Suede chokers decorated with: (left to right) India ink with marking-pen outline, Marking pens, Glued suede appliques, India ink with marking-pen outline, Stitched suede appliqués, India ink with marking-pen outline, India ink with marking-pen outline, p. 54.

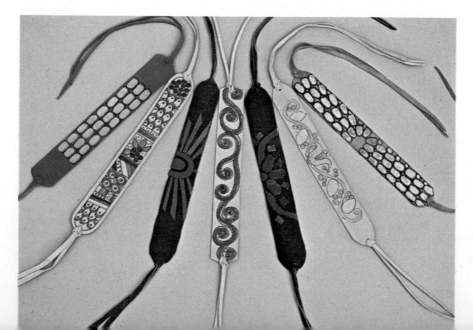

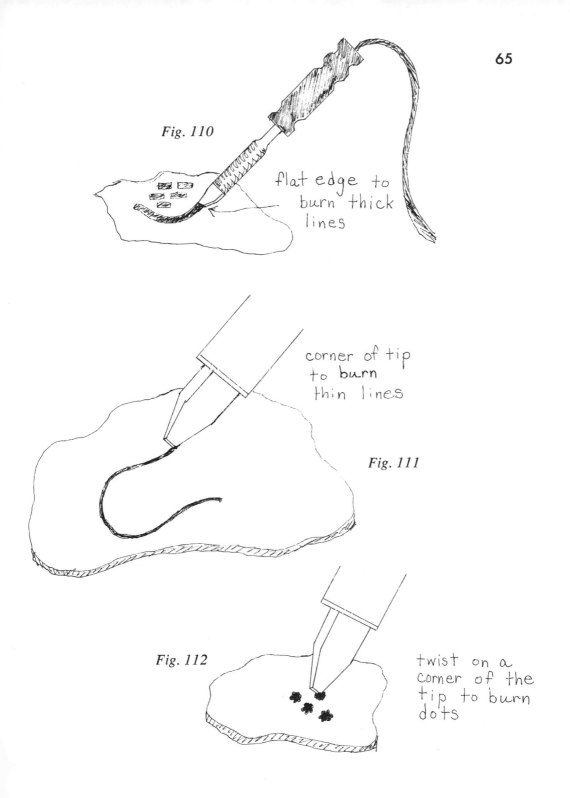

Fig. 110

flat edge to
burn thick
lines

corner of tip
to burn
thin lines

Fig. 111

Fig. 112

twist on a
corner of the
tip to burn
dots

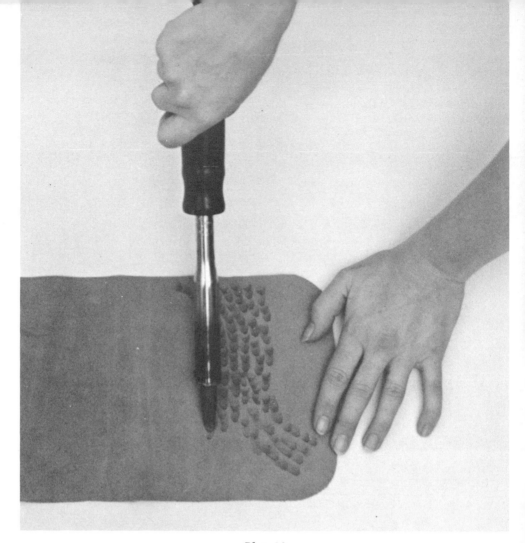

Plate 18

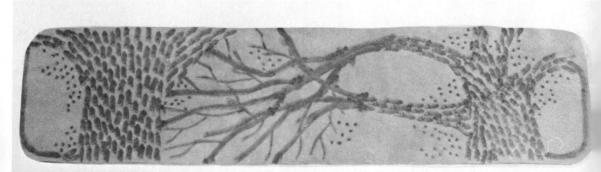

Plate 19

ATTACHING HOOKS

Position your hooks evenly on each front edge with the hook portion down. Mark through each hole with a pen (fig. 113). Punch out each hole with smallest hole on the punch. Cut 2 very thin thongs 3/16-inch wide and 12-inches long. Point one end only. Starting at one edge of the belt and on the wrong side, thread through the first hook hole and suede hole simultaneously. Leave about ½-inch of the unpointed end loose on the wrong side, to be glued down later. Now thread down through the next suede hole and hook hole (fig. 114). Keep going until you've threaded five hooks on each of the front edges. Clip both ends of the thong to about ½-inch (fig. 115). Glue these ends down. You may have to hold them down by hand until they dry.

Now paste on the Pellon backing. Pay special attention to gluing the Pellon where the hooks are. Weight these ends down with heavy objects while they're drying. Cut 1 thong 36-inches long for the cross lacing. Lace it onto the hooks (plate 20).

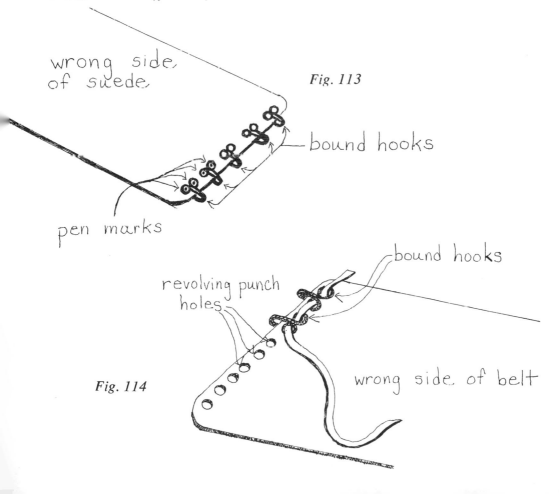

wrong side of suede

Fig. 113

bound hooks

pen marks

revolving punch holes

bound hooks

Fig. 114

wrong side of belt

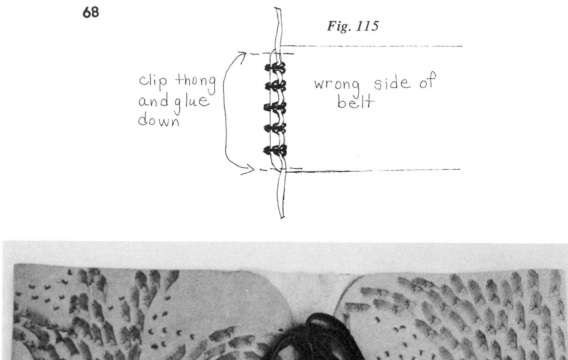

Fig. 115

clip thong
and glue
down

wrong side of
belt

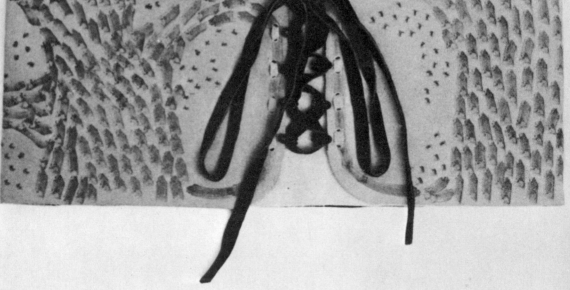

Plate 20

SUEDE BELT WITH GLUED APPLIQUES

As this belt is made in five sections, it could be made from scraps from a previous project. Shapes from contrasting colored scraps will be pasted on these sections to create your design. Unless you already have scrap pieces, you will have to locate a shop that sells them.

MATERIALS

    Suede lambskin (used here: purple)
    Suede scraps (used here; light dusty pink, dark dusty pink, olive green,
       plum)
    Pellon
    Scissors
    Leather glue
    Ruler or steel straightedge
    Masking tape
    Revolving punch

Whether you use scraps or one large piece, you must figure out the proportion of your pieces. You will need ½-inch extra on each overlapping edge. With five pieces you will have eight overlapping edges (fig. 116). This will mean 4 extra inches altogether. Add these 4-inches to your waist measurement. You can, of course, cut your pieces into any proportion you like. To duplicate the belt made here, cut two 2-inch pieces, 4-inches wide. Divide the remaining measurement into three equal parts (fig. 117). Make each of these pieces, 4-inches wide.

    Paste Pellon on back of each piece. Round off all corners. To obtain uniform curves, cut the curve on one corner. Then fold your first piece in half, matching ends and trace the curve (fig. 118). Fold the same piece in

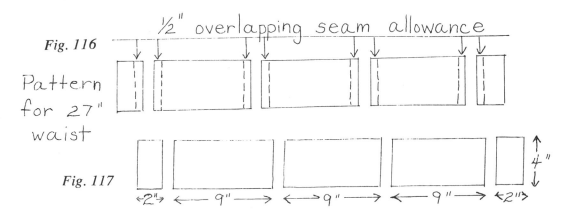

Fig. 116

Pattern for 27" waist

½" overlapping seam allowance

Fig. 117

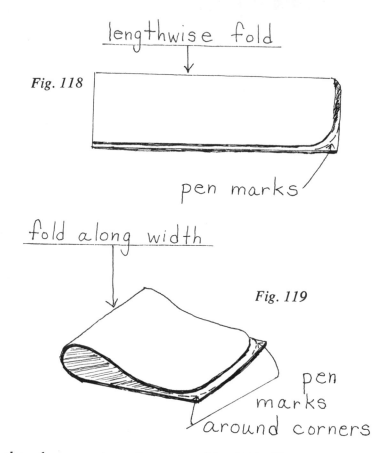

lengthwise fold

Fig. 118

pen marks

fold along width

Fig. 119

pen marks around corners

half the other way; trace the curves (fig. 119). Trace these curves on all other pieces.

FITTING THE BELT

Take a piece of masking tape the same size as your waist measurement and tape it to the straightedge of your work table. Working from the tape edges towards the center of the tape, place each 2-inch piece at each end of your masking tape line. Keep the pieces within the masking tape. Place two of the remaining pieces inside the tape line but overlapping the first two pieces by ½-inch. Place the last piece in the middle, overlapping these last two larger pieces (fig. 120). If you find that this last piece overlaps much more than the first two pieces, adjust them so all edges overlap evenly.

Pick up the middle piece without disturbing the other pieces. Fold it in half, matching edges (fig. 121). Punch 4 holes through both thicknesses, using the second largest hole on your punch. These holes are to be used to join your pieces together. If you can't do it by eye, use a ruler to mark the

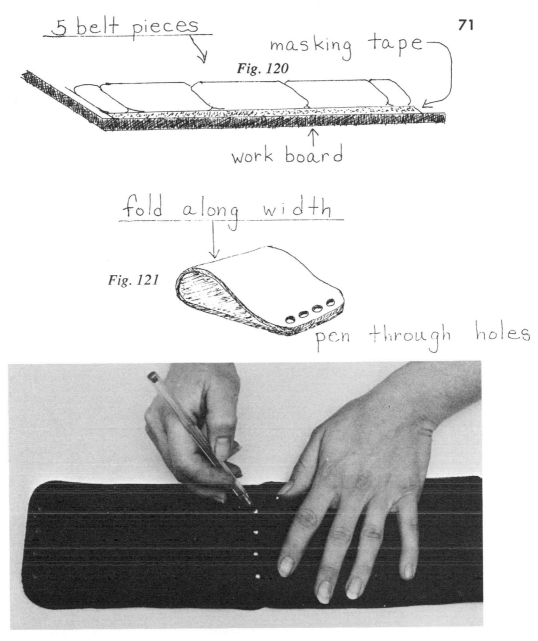

5 belt pieces

Fig. 120

masking tape

work board

fold along width

Fig. 121

pen through holes

Plate 21

place to punch. Open the piece. Place it back where it was. Mark through all the holes (plate 21). You now have marks on each edge of the next two pieces. Punch them out (plate 21).

Fig. 122

JOINING BELT SECTIONS WITH THONGS

Cut 4 very thin thongs 3/16-inch wide and about 14-inches long. Make a point on both ends of each thong. Make a knot about 1-inch in, on only one end of each thong. Working with the back piece and one side piece, line up the holes. Double one thong so that the points are together (fig. 122). Push both points through the first set of holes, from the right side to the wrong side (plate 22). Pull both ends through until there is no more slack left on the right side of the suede. You'll be left with one long and one short end on the wrong side. Only the knot will remain on the right side. Using the long thong end, thread it up through the next set of holes. Once on the right side again, knot the thong as tightly as you can. Holding this part of the belt in your hand, pull the knot towards you so you can see through the hole a little. Push the thong (now knotted) back through this hole (plate 23). Do the same for the next two holes, ending up on the wrong side of the belt. Cut off the excess thong on each end, leaving enough to paste down (plate 24). Mark holes and thong with knots the same way on all remaining overlapping edges. On the front edges you can use any thonging method you like. Because I felt it carried out the design, I chose the knotted method. This required eight 18-inch thongs and four double rows of holes on each front edge.

Plate 22

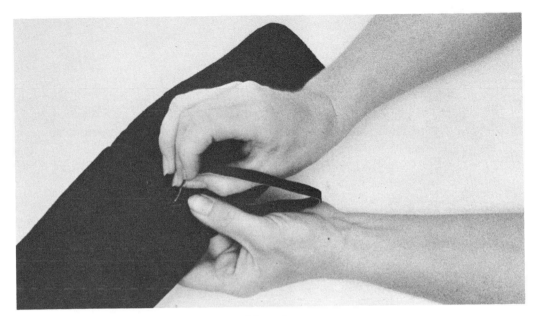

Plate 23

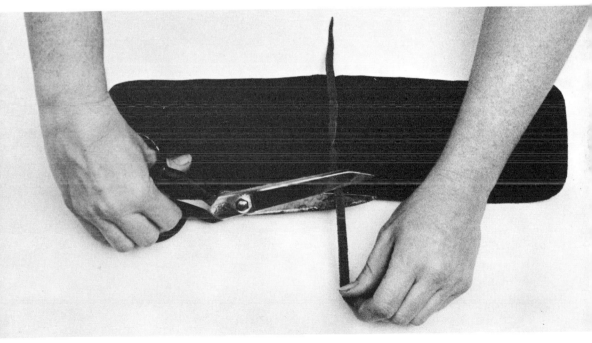

Plate 24

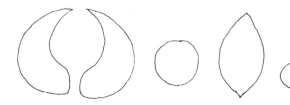

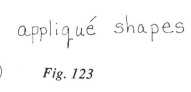

appliqué shapes

Fig. 123

Making The Appliques

Because this belt is sectioned, it lends itself to a repeat pattern. Limit yourself to four or five simple shapes (fig. 123). You may want to cut shapes out of paper first. Once you've decided what shapes you're using, trace them onto your suede scraps (plate 25). For harmony of design, I made all the same shapes the same color. If you wish to reverse a shape, you simply flip your pattern (fig. 124).

Cut out all your shapes and place them on each panel. Do not paste until all your pieces are cut and in place (plate 26). This gives you a chance to move them around, trim pieces, if necessary, or change your mind.

When you like the effect, pick up one piece at a time without disturbing the others, and holding it flat on your fingertips, apply glue to the wrong side. If you lay it down, or apply glue too close to the edges, there is danger of the glue running onto the right side and marring the suede (plate 27).

Plate 25

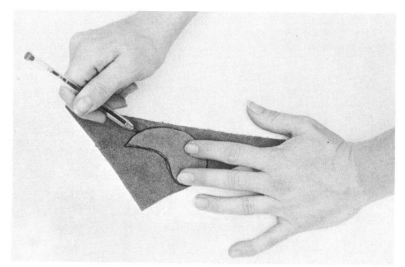

Plate 26

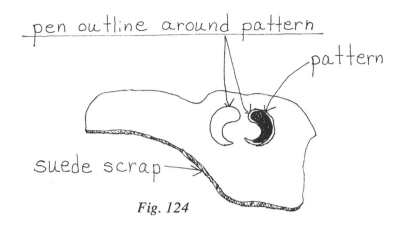

pen outline around pattern

pattern

suede scrap

Fig. 124

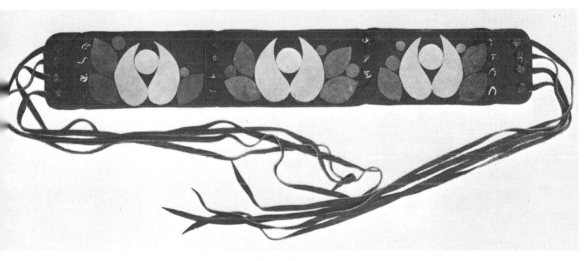

Plate 27

SUEDE BELT WITH STITCHED APPLIQUE

The construction of this belt is almost identical to the belt made in the last project.

MATERIALS

    Suede skin
    Suede scraps in 2 colors
    Button tacks
    Embroidery thread (used here: black)
    Large-eyed needle
    Scissors
    Leather glue
    Ruler or steel straightedge
    Pellon
    Revolving punch

On your suede, mark off your waist size plus 2 extra inches for the length of the belt. Make it 4-inches wide. Divide this length into three equal parts (fig. 125). Round off the corners. Using the smallest hole on the punch, punch 3 holes on the ends of one piece. This will be the back piece. Place all three pieces within the masking tape line as you did in the last project. The piece with the holes in it goes between the other two, and overlapping them. Fit all pieces within the tape line (fig. 126). Mark through the holes and punch, using the smallest hole. Do not put the pieces together now. Do not punch holes for the thongs.

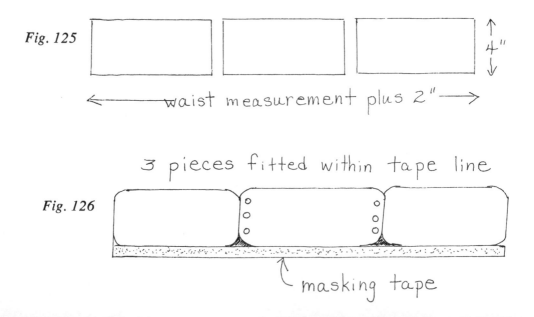

Fig. 125

⟵ waist measurement plus 2" ⟶

4"

3 pieces fitted within tape line

Fig. 126

masking tape

MAKING APPLIQUES

Cut your appliqué pieces, keeping in mind that they will not touch each other. Do not place any piece too close to the edge holes or to the outside edges. Remember you have two pieces overlapping and you don't want any appliquéd pieces covered when you put the edges together. Decide what kind of thonging you'll use and leave enough empty space for them. When you've arranged all your appliqué pieces, paste them on, one at a time.

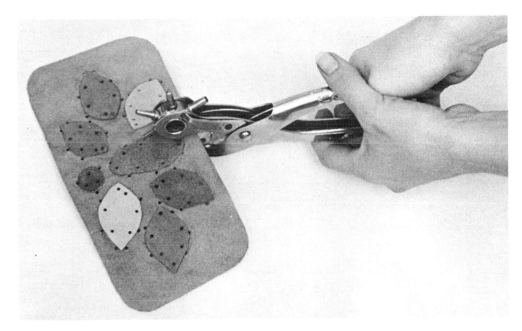

Plate 28

STITCHING AROUND APPLIQUES

Your first step, before punching the holes for the stitching, should be to study the appliquéd pattern as it will appear when finished (plate 30). Then, with the smallest hole on your revolving punch, punch holes around and on each pasted piece. Punch 1 hole near the edge of one piece but not on the edge. Punch the next hole a little further away and on the appliqué piece but close to its edge. The next hole should be off the appliqué piece, but close to the second hole (plate 28). Continue doing this alternating on the piece, then off the piece, until you've punched around each pasted appliquéd piece. Be sure you end with the same number of holes on the appliqué piece as off. If you do happen to have one hole too many, punch another one either above or below the last one. Thread the needle with embroidery thread. Double it. Tie a big knot at the end. If the knot is too small it will slip through the holes. Starting on the wrong side, stitch around each piece (plate 29). If you've sewn before, you already know that if you make your thread too long it will get tangled. The safest length is no longer than the distance from your fingertips to your nose with your arm stretched out. Better to use many shorter threads than one very long one (plate 30).

Plate 29

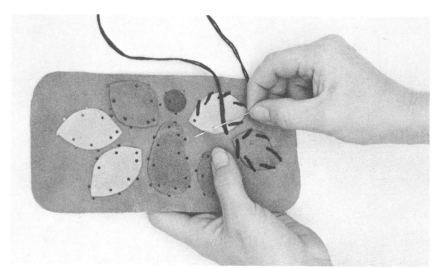

Plate 30

When you've finished stitching, paste Pellon to the back of each belt section. Keep the Pellon flat on your table. Apply the glue to it and place your suede piece on top of that. Press down gently. Pressing down too hard may make the glue ooze through the holes.

BUTTON TACKS

To attach the button tacks, simply push the tack portion through the Pellon and up through the suede hole. Place the head (button part) on top and press down firmly (fig. 127).

Punch holes for the thongs on the front edges. This time, I chose knot thonging because I didn't have enough scrap left for the double length I needed to make longer ones (plate 31).

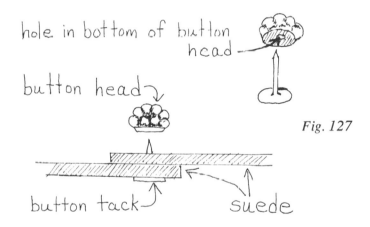

Fig. 127

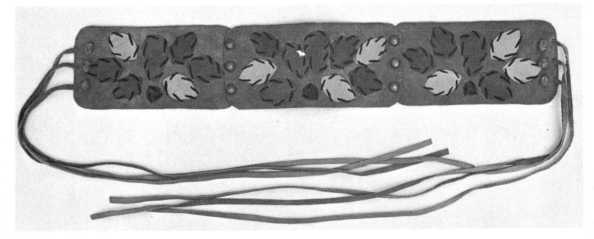

Plate 31

SHORT BOLERO

The first time you make a fitted piece of clothing, use a purchased pattern. Choose a simple one in your exact size, with no more than bust darts. McCall's pattern #9689 was used here. The back darts were eliminated by cutting ½-inch off the back of the armhole at the shoulder seam.

MATERIALS

   Suede skin (used here; rust)
   Leather skin (used here: dark brown cabretta)
   Revolving punch
   Scissors

Lay the back of the pattern on the suede. Use double-faced masking tape to keep your pattern piece in place; or simply weight it down with something heavy. Avoid using pins; they will leave holes. Cut it ½-inch larger on each side and shoulder seam (fig. 128). This extra is needed in order to thong the pieces together.

   Cut the front pieces from the leather skin. Place your pattern carefully to be sure you'll get two pieces out of it, and that you'll also avoid any holes or mars. Cut out along the dart lines, removing this area of leather completely (plate 32).

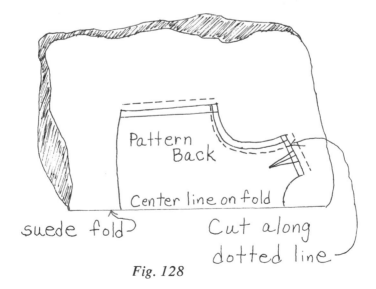

Fig. 128

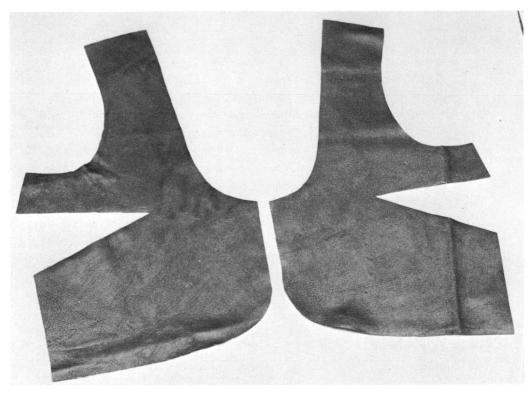

Plate 32

LACING DARTS AND SEAMS

Fold the dart edges together. Starting slightly above the dart point, punch 9 holes along the dart edge using the third largest hole on the punch. Your last hole should end 1¼-inches from the side seam (fig. 129). Cut 6 thongs from the cabretta ¼-inch wide and long enough to be laced through all the holes on each seam, with some to spare. Cut points on all ends. Start cross-lacing the darts on the right side of the leather by pulling the thong ends down through the first set of holes (plate 33). Cross them and push them up through the next set of holes. Cross on the right side and push them down through the next set. Continue, ending on the wrong side.

On the front pieces, punch a double row of holes on each shoulder and side seam. Punch five sets of holes on each shoulder and seven sets on each side seam. Lay your back piece out flat, right side up. Place your front pieces, right side up, overlapping the back piece at the shoulder seams. Be sure all holes overlap the edges by ¼-inch. Do not be disturbed if the back armhole or neck edge is larger than the front. This can be trimmed off later.

Mark through the holes. Now place the front pieces over the back at the side seams. Mark through the holes again. Punch out all holes (plate 34). With side seam edges overlapping and holes lined up, start on the inside and push the thongs up through one set of matching holes (fig. 130). Cross the laces on the right side of the bolero and thread through the appropriate holes and cross them again on the back. Continue crossing thongs and lacing into the next hole diagonally across from it. End with the loose ends of the thongs on the outside and tie (plate 35).

To finish the bolero cross-lace all seams. Cut the excess off the dart thongs and paste the end down flat, inside.

Add 2 thongs to the front top corners by punching 2 holes on each corner and lacing 1 thong through each set (fig. 131 and plate 36).

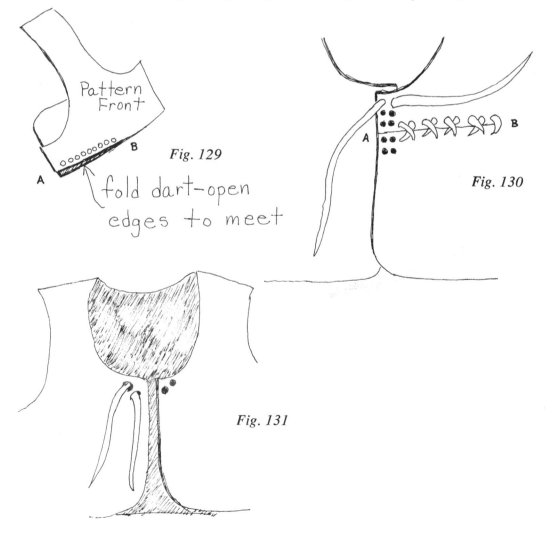

Fig. 129

fold dart-open edges to meet

Fig. 130

Fig. 131

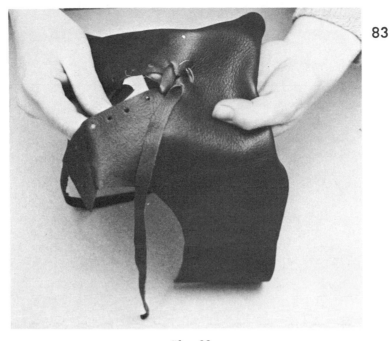

Plate 33

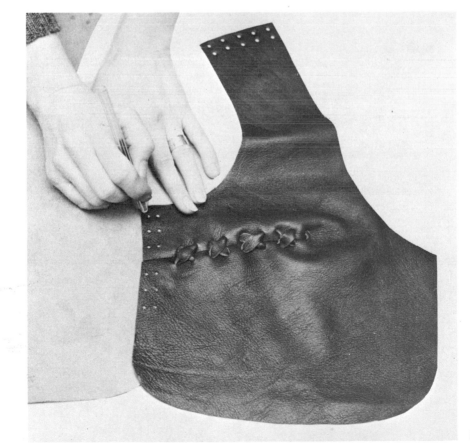

Plate 34

Plate 35

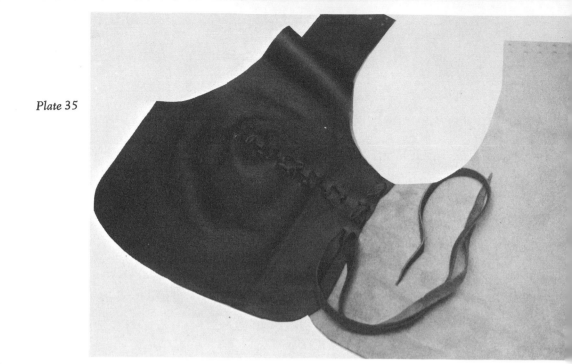

Plate 36

WAIST-LENGTH SUEDE VEST

MATERIALS

> Split suede cowhide (used here: olive green)
> Lamb suede (used here: lime green)
> India inks in white and choice of colors (used here: ultramarine blue)
> Black marking pen
> Scissors
> Brushes
> Leather glue (used here: Du-All Super #88)

Whenever you use any type of liquid coloring you should be aware that the color of the leather or suede will change the colors of your paint or inks. If you choose to make this vest with colors other than those used here, you may have to experiment on a scrap of the same suede, before you achieve an effect you like. Sometimes interesting colors can be obtained by using only the three primary colors, red, yellow and blue; and painting one color over another. To get cleaner colors and to cut down on the color changing, try white ink under your colors. This procedure also cuts down on absorption. Because ink is a wetter coloring than, for instance, an oil base paint, it is absorbed into the suede more thoroughly and the inks change more drastically. Usually it is a muted color compared to the fresh ink in the bottle.

When cutting leather or suede, be sure you do not cut it too small. It would be better to cut your pieces slightly larger and trim them down later, if necessary. Using Simplicity pattern #8300, cut your pieces to pattern specifications. Glue them together at the shoulder and at side seams (plate 37).

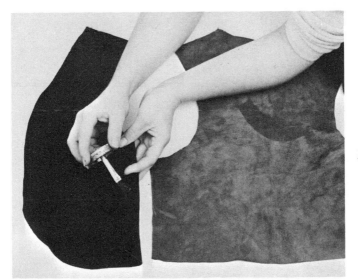

Plate 37

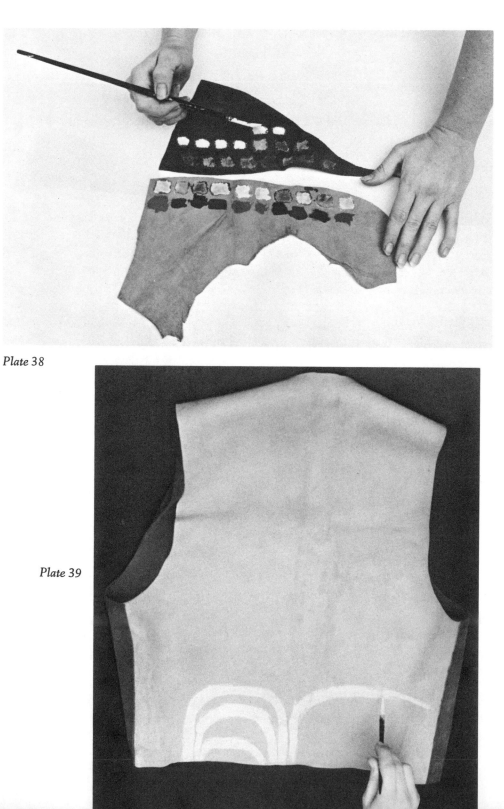

Plate 38

Plate 39

INDIA INKS ON SUEDE

Test your colors on a swatch of each kind of suede. Try the colors alone and then with white underneath (plate 38). Let them dry so you can see the final color. Starting on the back of the vest, use a paintbrush to apply the white ink (plate 39). When dry, paint over it with ultramarine blue (or your choice of color). In my vest, the outer edges were allowed to catch some of the blue and, in some cases, were purposely painted with it to create contrast. Outline some areas with the black marking pen if you like. You will have to use your own judgment about where it looks best. My design was brushed on very freely without worrying about neat edges or filled-in areas (plate 40).

On lamb suede of any color, India inks, when applied without white ink underneath, are almost always colorless.

On cowhide, white ink used under any color, will often result in a fluorescent look.

Plate 40

FRINGED VEST

MATERIALS

> 1 sheet brown butcher paper or 2 large sheets of newspaper
> 3 split suede cowhides
> Steel straightedge
> Mat knife with extra blades
> Heavy backing board, 20 x 30-inches
> Chalk
> Scissors
> Crow beads (fat, squat, plastic beads with a large hole)

MAKING A PATTERN

Use the brown paper to make your own pattern.

1. To begin, measure across your back from side seam to side seam, 2-inches below the armpit (fig. 132). Divide this measurement in half. Rule this new measurement across the width of the paper (fig. 133).

2. Measure from the base of your neck to the desired length of the vest (fig. 134). Rule this measurement along the length of the paper (fig. 135). You now have a big rectangle.

3. Measure across your neck, from shoulder seam to shoulder seam (fig. 136). Divide the neck measurement in half. Mark this length, measuring from the edge of your paper in. This edge is the center back line.

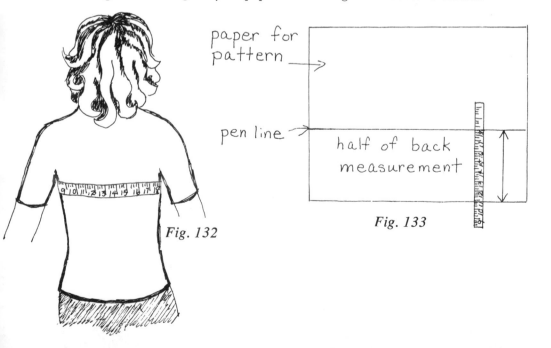

paper for pattern

pen line

half of back measurement

Fig. 132

Fig. 133

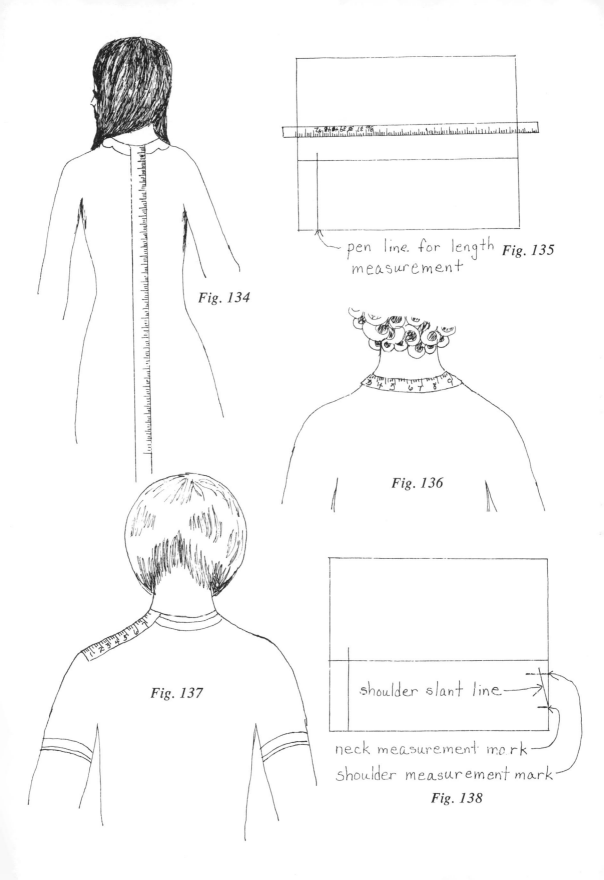

Fig. 134

pen line for length
measurement   Fig. 135

Fig. 136

Fig. 137

shoulder slant line

neck measurement mark
shoulder measurement mark
Fig. 138

4. Measure across the top of one shoulder (fig. 137). From the neck mark, measure towards the line in the center of your paper. Draw a line the length of your shoulder measurement, slanting down to 1-inch lower at the pen line (fig. 138).

5. Draw the neck curve by starting at the neck mark and curving down to 1-inch lower at the outer edge of paper.

6. Measure straight down from the edge of your shoulder to 2 inches below the armpit (fig. 139). Mark this from the lower slanted edge of your shoulder line along the side seam pen line. Draw the armhole curve. Notice that the deepest part of the curve will fit under your arm (fig. 140). Estimate this curve, leaving more suede than you think necessary. You can always cut off the excess later.

7. For the pattern front, measure across your bust or chest from side seam to side seam. Divide this measurement in half. Rule this across the width of your paper from the other edge (fig. 141). Rule the length on the paper the same way you did the back.

8. Mark the neck and shoulder measurements as you marked the back. Fill in the armhole curve.

9. To draw the front opening start at the inside shoulder mark. Rule your line diagonally to a point adjacent to the top of the side seam (fig. 142). Cut your pattern and place it on the suede.

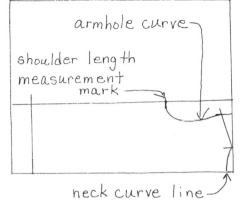

Fig. 140

armhole curve

shoulder length measurement mark

neck curve line

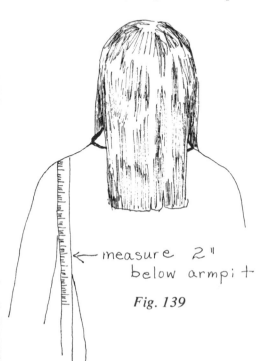

measure 2" below armpit

Fig. 139

Fig. 141

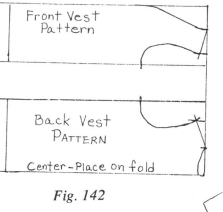

Front Vest Pattern

Back Vest PATTERN

Center-Place on fold

Fig. 142

Fig. 143

5"

vest front

chalk line

chalk line

CUTTING THE VEST

Working the same as always, on the wrong side of the suede, cut 2 fronts. To cut the back, fold one piece of suede in half the long way. Place the center back of the pattern on the fold and cut, making one single back section.

On each front section measure 5-inches down from the armhole edge. Draw a straight line at this mark across the inside of both front sections with chalk (fig. 143). This line marks where the fringe begins.

Lay your steel straightedge at a right angle to this chalk line and about ¼-inch from the edge furthest away from you. This will be the first fringe. Cut fringes ¼-inch wide. With your mat knife cut along the edge of the steel ruler (plate 41). As you pull your mat knife down the edge, press firmly to hold the ruler in place. Cut only along the portion held down by your fingers.

Plate 41

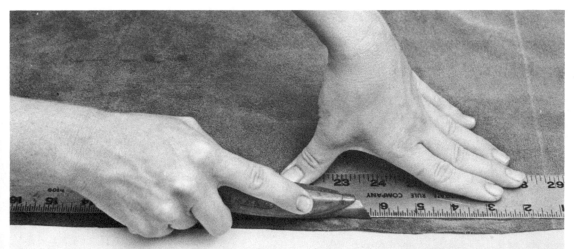

Do not cut any further until you have moved your fingers adjacent to the area you will cut next. Press firmly on the mat knife but do not force the blade too much or the suede will crimp (cut in wavy lines). Your blade will penetrate less of the thickness as it becomes duller. It's advisable to change blades often since they dull quickly. Do not be concerned if you can't cut all the way through. Later you can finish cutting through these partially cut lines with scissors (plate 42).

The back will be cut to a "V" shape. Working on the wrong side, again measure down 5 inches from each armhole opening and mark with chalk. Measure across to the center back 2 inches lower than this measurement and mark. Use your steel edge to connect these 3 marks (fig. 144).

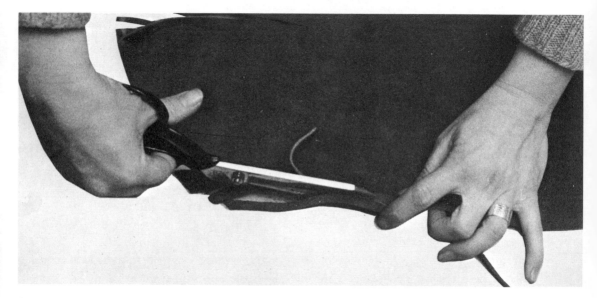

Plate 42

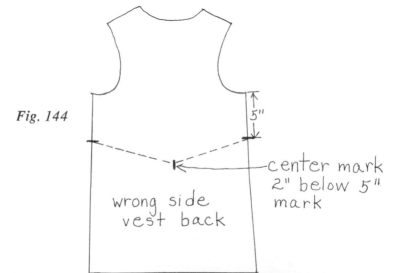

Fig. 144

5"

center mark
2" below 5"
mark

wrong side
vest back

A word of caution: when you're cutting the fringe and approach the edge nearest you, you'll notice that the suede starts slipping from under the ruler. This happens because there isn't enough suede left to put pressure on. Simply stop cutting with the mat knife and finish cutting the fringe with the scissors.

Lace the sides and shoulders together by using double rows of holes and either cross-lacing or using the thongs to make a running stitch (plate 43).

From your scrap, cut 12 fringes of varying lengths and cut a point in both ends. Punch pairs of holes near the front edges. Slip the fringes through the holes and let them hang (plate 44).

BEADING

The last step is to add the beads. You can attach them in patterns (plate 45), or at random (plate 46). If you have difficulty pulling them on, trim the fringe thinner with scissors (plate 47).

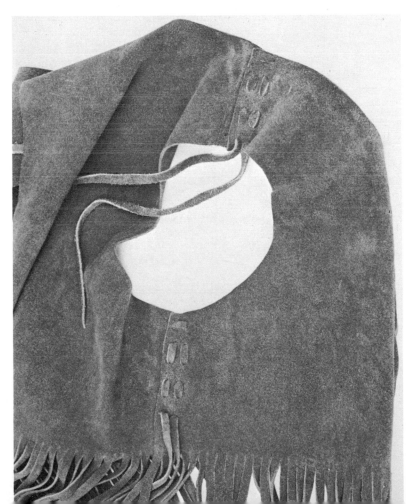

Plate 43

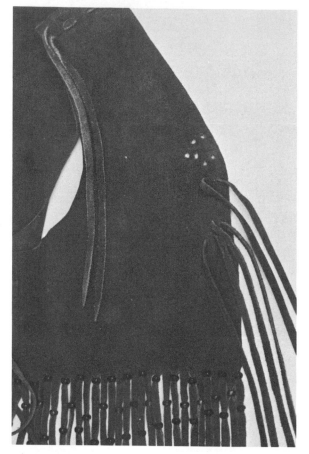

Plate 44

Plate 45

Plate 46

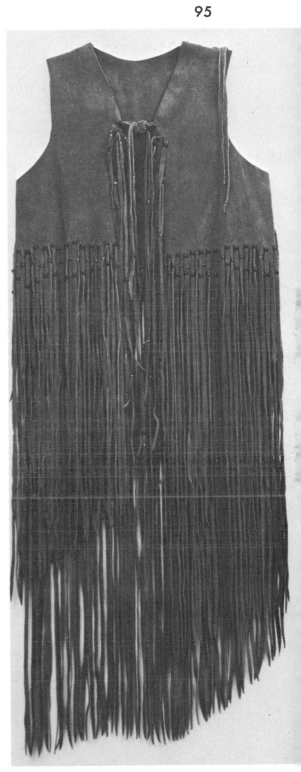

Plate 47

MACHINE-SEWN LEATHER VEST

When you buy the leather take your pattern pieces with you so you're sure to buy enough. This vest was adapted from Simplicity pattern #8469; by eliminating the sleeves and redesigning the front.

MATERIALS

    3 leather skins (used here; cabretta antique brown. If skins are small you may need one more)

    Lining (same amount as for the vest)

    Scissors

    Leather glue (used here: Du-All Super #88)

    No. 50 mercerized thread

    Tissue paper (preferably with one side slightly shiny)

    Brown paper strips

    Sewing machine

    Singer sewing machine needles for leather

    Straight pins

When cutting cabretta and other loose, stretchable leathers, you must lay your pattern along the length of the leather, from the neck to the tail. If you can't tell which end is which, look for the footage mark on the wrong side. This mark is always at the tail end (fig. 145). If you cut it in any other direction your garment will stretch out of shape. Each pattern piece will have an arrow indicating the straight of the cloth. Lay this arrow along the length of the leather from the neck to the tail.

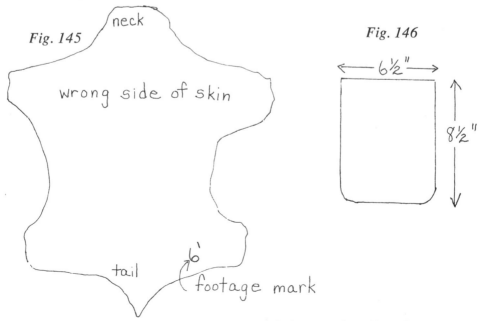

Fig. 145

neck

wrong side of skin

tail

footage mark

Fig. 146

6½"

8½"

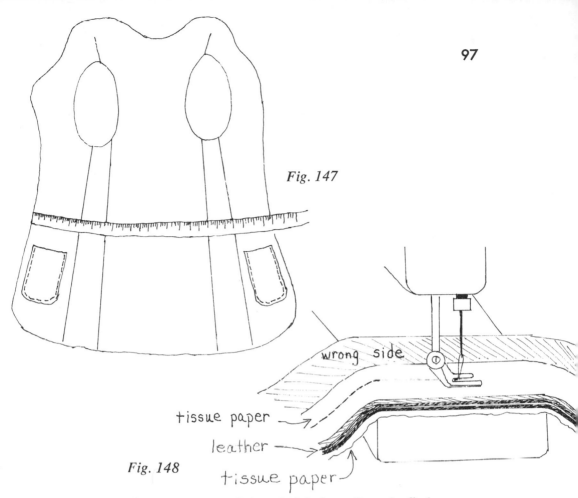

Fig. 147

Fig. 148

wrong side

tissue paper

leather

tissue paper

Cut pockets from the scrap, 6½ x 8½-inches. Round off the two bottom edges (fig. 146).

Cut the belt after the vest shell has been sewn together but before the lining has been put in, by measuring across the vest (fig. 147).

Machine-stitch front sections to back, sewing seams according to pattern directions. When machine sewing on the wrong side of leather, use tissue paper over and under your work. But, when sewing on the right side, use heavy brown paper strips because they rip away cleaner. Tissue paper will leave tiny white fragments which are difficult to remove. Using paper, you'll find, will help the leather move smoothly through the machine without pulling (fig. 148). Press open shoulder and side seams with your fingers and glue down (plate 48). When machine stitching, try to do it right the first time, any holes you make are permanent and will mark the leather. If you have to rip out and resew, it may result in tearing the vest since each time you puncture the leather you make a potential weak spot.

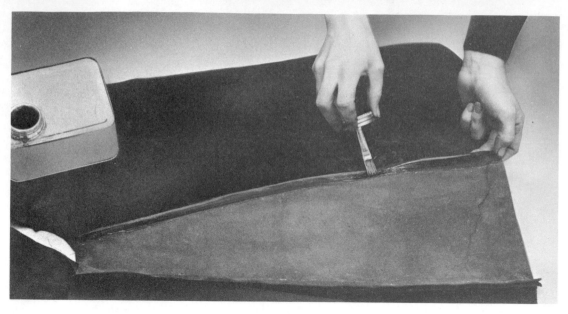

Plate 48

Stay stitch, using a large stitch, around the neck and armhole edges ⅝-inch from the edge. Clip the leather along these curves almost to the stay stitching. Fold under and glue down (fig. 149). Glue the bottom hemline and front edges, rippling the seam allowance (which won't show) to take up the excess around the curve (fig. 150). Be careful that you do not stretch the leather as you do this.

Fold the top edge of the pocket down 1-inch and stitch ¼-inch from this fold. Clip the flap edge inward from the stitching (fig. 151). Place the pockets on the vest fronts. Stitch around the sides and bottom leaving the top edge free (fig. 152).

If you do not have enough length to cut the belt in one piece, cut it in two equal pieces and sew them together. Place the belt where you want it and glue down lightly. This will keep it from slipping when you sew. Stitch it on.

Cut 6 thongs, each ¼ x 17 inches. Glue them along the front edge with the right sides of the thongs facing the wrong side of the vest. Place one on each side at the top edge and two on each side at the belt edges (fig. 153).

LINING

Cut your lining the same size as your vest. Sew the pieces together. Iron the seams open. Stay-stitch around the neck and armholes, ½ inch from the edges. Clip the armhole and neck curves almost to the stay-stitching. To fit the lining, pin the leather shoulder seam to the lining shoulder seam, folding in the lining edges as you go. The lining edge will be slightly inside the leather edge (fig. 154). Pin the lining around the back of the neck and armhole edges, folding it in as you go. Then, pin the lining seams to the leather seams. Make sure you're not moving the lining too far up or down on the leather seam lines, by matching pattern notches. Spread the vest out to be sure it is not pulling across the back. The lining should be slightly larger than the vest. Pin the lining front neck edges and front opening edges to the leather. Keep the vest front spread out as you do so, again to be sure it is not pulling in the wrong direction. Turn the vest inside out and try it on for comfort (plate 49). When you do this you can see if there is any pulling, and correct it by re-pinning.

With lining facing you and leather face down on the machine, stitch the lining to the vest around the armholes and neck and down the front edges to within 3-inches of the bottom. Use the same length stitch you used around the pockets and belt. Try to keep your stitching an even distance from all edges. Remove all pins including those holding the lining seams to the leather seams.

Fold the lining in around the bottom edge, from the front curves, and all around the hemline. Pin in place. Once again, spread out the vest to be sure it's not pulling. Machine stitch all remaining lining edges in place.

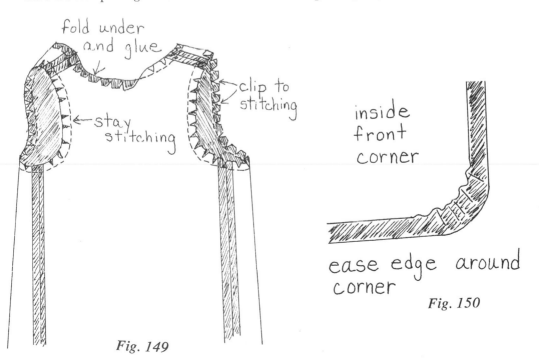

fold under and glue

clip to stitching

stay stitching

inside front corner

ease edge around corner

Fig. 150

Fig. 149

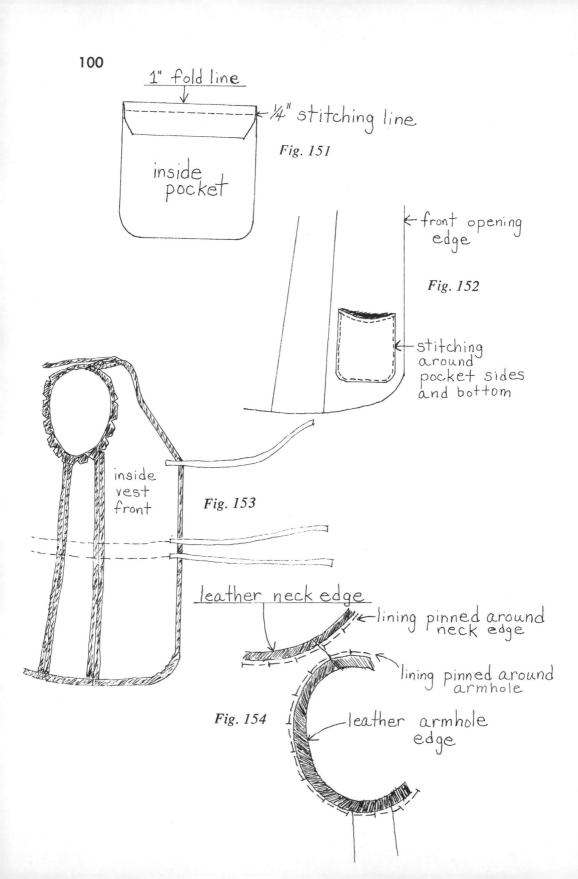

1" fold line

¼" stitching line

inside pocket

Fig. 151

front opening edge

Fig. 152

stitching around pocket sides and bottom

inside vest front

Fig. 153

leather neck edge

lining pinned around neck edge

lining pinned around armhole

leather armhole edge

Fig. 154

Plate 49

SUEDE SKIRT

MATERIALS

> 1 large split suede cowhide
> 5-prong stitching chisel
> 2 harness needles
> 5-ply waxed thread
> Wood board
> Mallet (wood or rawhide)
> Leather glue
> Scissors

MAKING A PATTERN FROM AN OLD GARMENT

The easiest skirt to make is one which sits on your hips. This skirt was cut from an old four-gore skirt. Without taking it apart, a paper pattern was made by folding the skirt along its seams, tracing it to exact size, and then adding ½ inch at each seam edge and 1 inch at the waist and hem edges. Only 4 pieces are necessary; 2 front and 2 back (fig. 155).

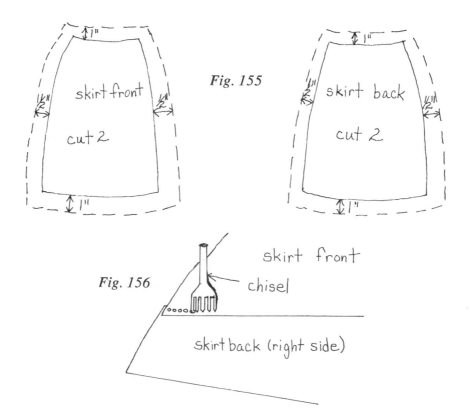

Fig. 155

skirt front cut 2

skirt back cut 2

Fig. 156

skirt front

chisel

skirt back (right side)

Plate 50

Using A Stitching Chisel

This skirt is made completely by hand. Working with the two front pieces, match the center front edges by placing their right sides together. Starting 1-inch from the top edge, with your wood board under this seam, place your stitching chisel ¼-inch in from the seam edge and hit it very hard with the mallet. Be sure you get through both thicknesses. You may have to hit it more than once. After some practice you'll be able to tell when it has gone through (plate 50). To space the holes evenly, put the last prong of the chisel in the last hole you made (fig. 156). Continue this process until you reach the bottom edge of the seam line. Before holing the three remaining seams, sew this seam together. Thread both needles with a single length of thread, knotting them at one end.

HAND-STITCHING

This chisel cuts holes very close to each other. To make the stitching more noticeable, skip every other hole when sewing. Overlap these edges, lining up the holes. Start stitching on the wrong side by pushing one needle up through the first set of holes and the second needle up through the third set of holes. The first needle now goes down through the third set of holes (where the second needle just came up (fig. 157). The second needle goes down through the first set of holes. Continue in this way, skipping every other hole, until you get as close to the bottom as possible. End on the wrong side.

Repeat this process for the other two seams. When chiseling holes for the back seam, follow the same procedure, leaving 6- or 7-inches open at the top. Fold the top edge down 1-inch and glue. Cut the bottom edge even, fold up 1-inch and glue. Punch a single row of holes along each back opening edge. With a long thin thong, cross-lace the opening from the stitching upward (plate 51).

A zipper can be sewn in by hand if preferred. Make stitching holes with the chisel. Do not fold these opening edges under because they will become too bulky.

Add appliqués or paint a design on your skirt if you want to make it snappier.

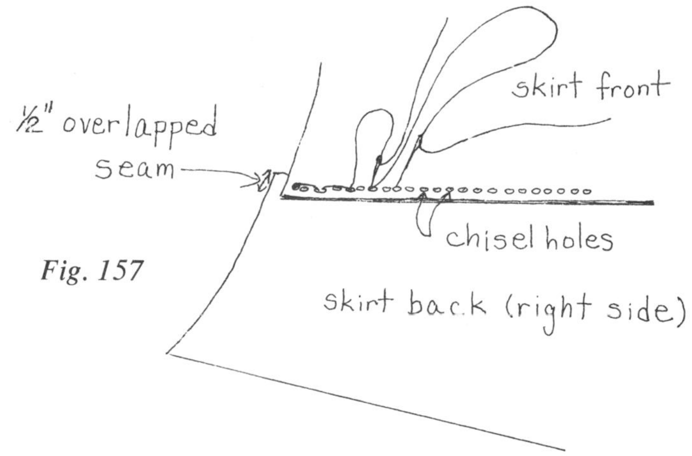

½" overlapped seam

skirt front

chisel holes

Fig. 157

skirt back (right side)

Plate 51

SUEDE TIE-DYED HOT PANTS AND MIDI VEST

MATERIALS

> 4 split suede cowhides each 8-square feet (used here: light blue, dyes will not show on darker colors)
> Two or three 12 x 18-inch pans, 3-inches deep
> Liquid dyes (used here: Rit evening blue and royal blue)
> Liquid detergent
> Eyelets
> Eyelet setter
> Rubber bands
> Scissors
> Leather glue
> 2 or more inexpensive ceiling tiles at least 24 x 48-inches (use both sides)
> Carpet tacks
> Hammer
> Heavy duty mercerized thread
> Sewing machine

TIE-DYEING

Work near a sink and four-burner stove. Soak all the pieces in cool water until fully saturated. Wring out the excess moisture and place one piece on a large flat surface. I used a ceiling tile as my work table.

Make 5 or 6 puckers by pinching the suede together (fig. 158). Wrap each pucker tightly with a rubber band (fig. 159).

To prepare the first dye bath, mix 5 tablespoons of evening blue liquid dye, 1 tablespoon liquid detergent and 1½-inches of hot tap water, in one of the pans. As you want your dye bath to be as hot as possible without boiling, always have your suede ready in advance. Liquid detergent helps the suede to absorb the color. Mix the dye bath on the stove without the burners on, so that it will be in the right spot when you dye your second piece (fig. 160). Place this first piece in the dye bath with the loose ends in the dye and the puckers up. Push the piece in the bath up to and including the rubber bands. Push the loose ends down gently with a spoon (or use rubber gloves if you want to keep your hands clean). Don't be too fussy about getting all the ends under; you'll get a more interesting effect by allowing the dye to swirl over some parts of the loose suede and not over others.

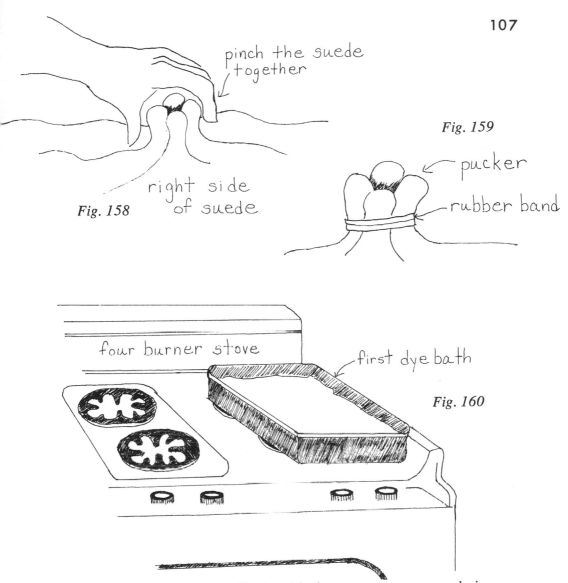

pinch the suede together

Fig. 159

pucker

rubber band

right side of suede

Fig. 158

four burner stove

first dye bath

Fig. 160

Let it sit for 30 minutes. During this time prepare your second piece of suede, puckering as you did before. After 30 minutes, take the first piece of suede out of the dye. Rinse it, without removing the rubber bands, in cool water until it runs clear. Prepare the second dye bath in the second pan by adding 3 tablespoons Rit liquid evening blue dye, plus 2 tablespoons navy blue dye and 1 tablespoon liquid detergent to 2-inches of hot tap water. Once again, prepare it on the stove over the burners, next to the first batch. Put the piece you just rinsed in this new dye bath, puckers down. At the same time, put your second piece of suede in the first dye bath, puckers up (fig. 161). Since this first dye bath is now cool, turn the flame on very low. When steam rises from the pan turn the burners off. Do not boil. Let both pieces sit for a total of 30 minutes.

When you take the first piece of suede out of the second bath, remove the rubber bands and rinse it thoroughly in cool water. Wring it as dry as possible. Spread the piece on a ceiling tile and nail it down with carpet tacks as close to the edge of the suede as possible. Stretch it taut, to remove wrinkles, as you nail it down (fig. 162).

Repeat this two-bath procedure for each piece of suede. After dyeing two pieces of suede, the dye baths are weak. Throw them out and mix two new batches for the next two pieces of suede. These last two pieces can be stretched on the opposite sides of the ceiling tiles already in use.

Let the suede dry thoroughly before untacking them. They should dry within one or two days. Do not try to rush the drying by putting them near heat, it might ruin your skins.

For hot pants, or any pants, you should use a pattern that has separate yoke pieces (fig. 163). The vest was adapted from Vogue's pattern #7888.

Fig. 161

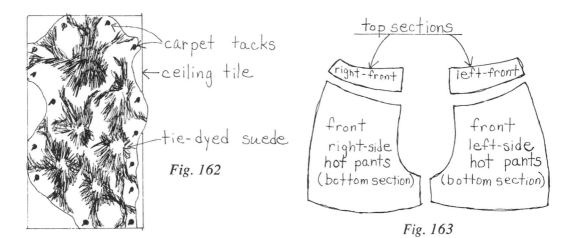

carpet tacks

ceiling tile

tie-dyed suede

Fig. 162

top sections

right-front

left-front

front
right-side
hot pants
(bottom section)

front
left-side
hot pants
(bottom section)

Fig. 163

MAKING THE VEST

Whenever there's any doubt about fit, I cut my pieces slightly larger all around. Then if it's too large, I can cut it down. Lay down all pattern pieces to be sure there's enough suede. Cut the vest first. Since this type of suede does not usually stretch very much, it's not important which way you cut it; you can cut the pants from leftover pieces. If the possibility of stretching worries you, then cut all pieces along the length of the suede. The pattern for the vest was adapted by lengthening it to 46 inches from the base of the neck. Two inches was cut off each shoulder seam (fig. 164), and the armholes were cut in deeper for a better fit. The vest back had to be cut in 3 pieces because there wasn't enough length to cut it from any one piece of suede (fig. 165).

Punch all the holes for this project with the third largest hole on the punch. Punch a single row of holes along each of the back center edges. You will have evenly matched holes if you punch through both pieces at the same time (fig. 166). Lace these top back pieces together by cross-lacing, ending on the wrong side of the garment (fig. 167). Punch a single row of holes along the bottom of this piece and a matching set along the top of the remaining back piece (fig. 168). Cross-lace these two pieces together with two separate thongs. Start from the middle and work out to the side seams, ending on the wrong side of the garment (fig. 169). Punch single rows of matching holes on the side and shoulder seams and on the front edge. Set eyelets in all these holes by pushing the eyelet down through the hole, from the right side to the wrong side, leaving the lipped edge on the right side (fig. 170). Use the eyelet setter to flatten out the eyelet and thus permanently fix it in place (fig. 171). If it is not flat enough on the wrong side, hammer it down lightly.

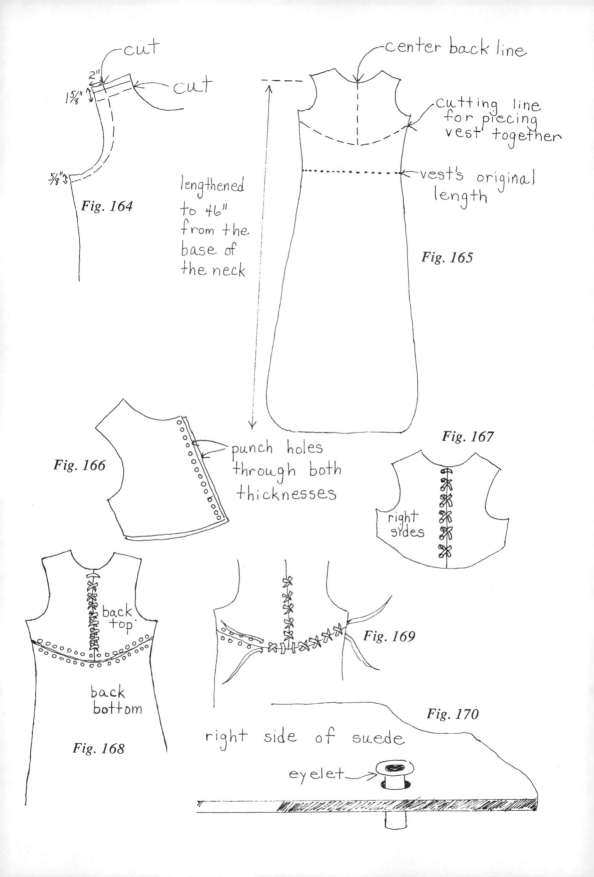

cut

2"

1 5/8"

cut

5/8"

Fig. 164

center back line

cutting line for piecing vest together

vest's original length

Fig. 165

lengthened to 46" from the base of the neck

Fig. 166

punch holes through both thicknesses

Fig. 167

right sides

back top

Fig. 169

back bottom

Fig. 168

Fig. 170

right side of suede

eyelet

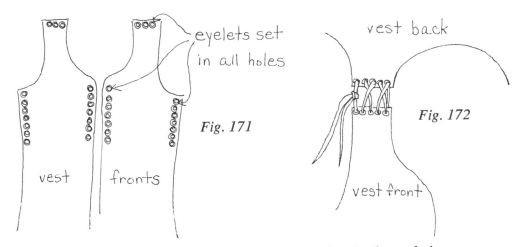

Fig. 171

Fig. 172

Cut 5 very thin thongs, making one very long for the front closing. Cut a point at both ends. Lace up the sides as you did the back pieces. If you like, leave the sides slightly open and cross-laced. When you lace the shoulder seams, leave the lacing loose and open (fig. 172). Cross your laces on top, but, on the underside, instead of crossing the opening, run the laces to the next hole on the same side. Lace the front in the same way.

Fit the vest. Cut the bottom edges even, and round off the corners.

MAKING THE HOT PANTS

Pants are always more difficult to make, because more fitting is involved. Because your pattern is sectioned into 8 pieces, you will get a good fit by adjusting the upper part of the side and back seams.

Start the pants by machine-sewing the two front pieces together along the crotch curve. Clip this curve to the stitching exactly as shown (fig. 173). Press open this seam with your fingers and stitch it flat. Repeat this procedure in stitching the two back bottom pieces together. Be sure you leave enough opening on both these pieces, especially the front, so you can get into them. Clip at the top of the stitching, on both front and back pieces, to the fold lines. Cut along both back seams, above the stitching along the fold lines to remove excess suede (fig. 174). Do the same to the right front opening, but leave a 1/4-inch flap on the left front. Machine-stitch the front inside leg seam to the back inside leg seam. Leave it as is. Do not open, clip or stitch down.

Lace the front top pieces to the front bottom pieces, starting from the center opening and working out to the side seams (fig. 175). The loose ends of your lacing should end on the outside of the pants and 3/4-inches from the side edge. Repeat for the back tops, leaving the last set of holes unlaced (fig.

176). Your lacing will end on the inside of the back of the pants. Lace the side seams from the bottom of the leg to within ½-inch of the top edge. At the point where the top section joins the bottom section, make certain that the top section is curved enough to conform to your body shape. End the lacing on the inside. Lace the back seam above the stitching using the same procedure. Once again, be sure you have curved the top sections to conform to your body shape.

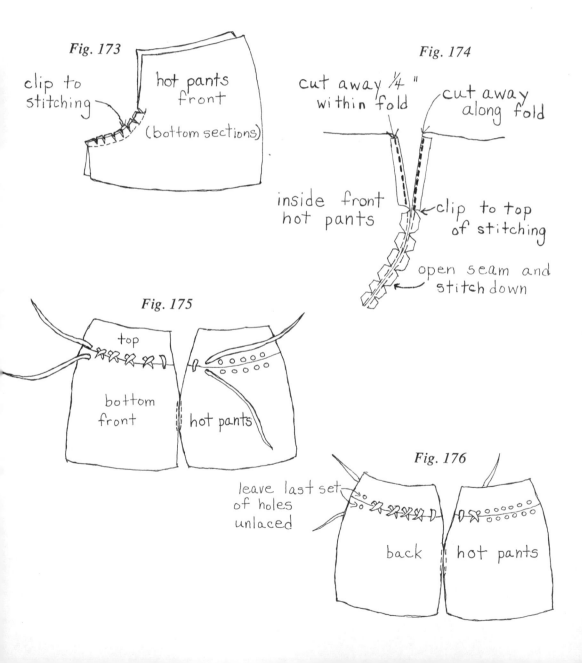

Fig. 173

clip to stitching

hot pants front

(bottom sections)

Fig. 174

cut away ¼" within fold

cut away along fold

inside front hot pants

clip to top of stitching

open seam and stitch down

Fig. 175

top

bottom front

hot pants

Fig. 176

leave last set of holes unlaced

back

hot pants

Punch matching sets of holes on the front opening, punching the left row of holes slightly further in than the right side. At the point along this edge where the top section joins the bottom, make sure your punch goes through both thicknesses (fig. 177). This will make for stronger construction. Fit with eyelets as before, leaving only the top holes on each side of the fly without eyelets. Cut a very thin thong, long enough to allow opening without pulling it out. Cut a 2-inch wide strip of suede from your scrap, slightly longer than the front opening. Glue it to the inside of the left front so that it will show when the pants are open. This flap will prevent whatever you're wearing under the pants from showing through the eyelet holes and the spaces between the lacing. Later when you fold down the top edge, you can insert the eyelet through both thicknesses.

Now try the pants for a final fitting. If they are too big around the waist, unlace the back center seam down to the seam that joins the top and bottom. Cut off the excess, tapering to this seam. Punch new holes and relace. You may find, as is usual, that your problem will not be solved by adjusting only this back seam. In fact, if you cut away too much, or taper too much, you'll be left with a funny little point where the four back sections meet. To avoid this, adjust the side seams as you did the back (fig. 178). No little bulges will appear, because the tapering will be less drastic if done on three seams instead of just one. Relace all seams. Repeat this process until you get a satisfactory fit.

Once you have the correct fit, you're ready for the finishing touches. The thongs joining the top front sections are now crossed over the side seam edges and laced into the last two holes on the back pieces.

Fig. 177

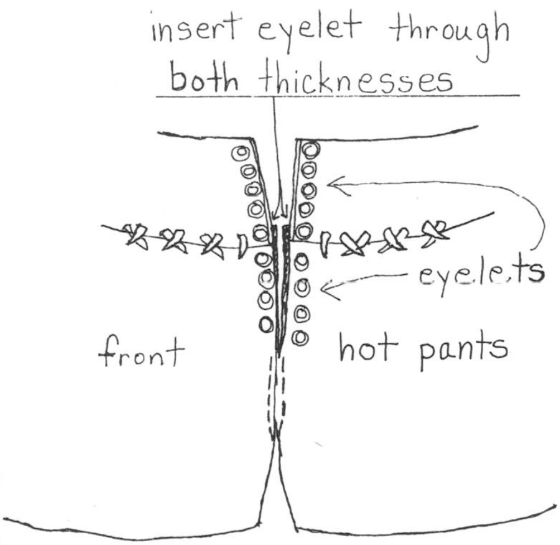

insert eyelet through both thicknesses

eyelets

front   hot pants

Fig. 178

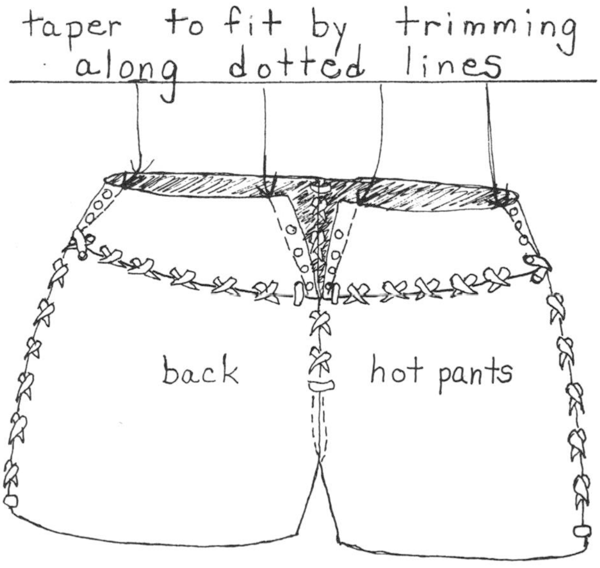

taper to fit by trimming along dotted lines

back   hot pants

From the top holes only, remove the lacing at three seams; the two sides and the center back. Fold the top edges down to the inside and glue (fig. 179). This will make your pants stronger at the top and less likely to stretch. Where this folded edge has covered the holes, punch through.

Re-lace. Cut these thong ends to 1½-inch lengths. Cross these ends on the inside and glue down. Crossing them pulls the open edges together. Cut all other thongs which ended on the inside of the pants, cross them over each other and glue down. Check all seam joinings. If any are not lying flat, carefully apply glue to hold them down (plate 52).

Long pants or a waist high skirt can also be made from heavy suede by using a pattern with yoke top. Patterns with darts can best be made with lightweight suedes or leathers. In this case, do not cut out the center of the dart. Instead, sew along the dart stitching lines, slash it through the middle to within ¼-inch of the point, fold and glue open (plate 53).

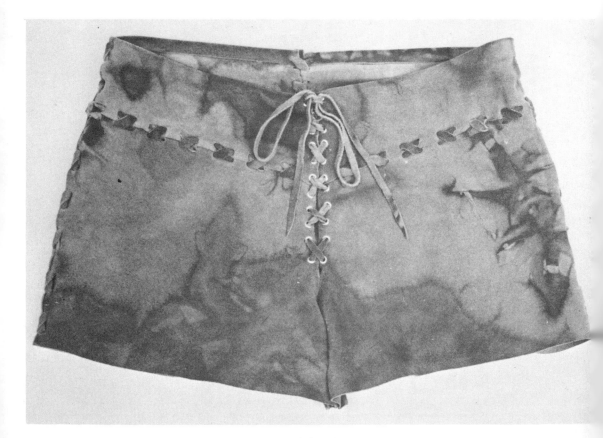

Plate 52

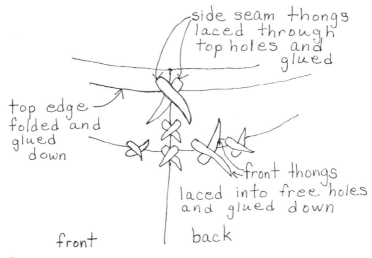

side seam thongs
laced through
top holes and
glued

top edge
folded and
glued
down

front thongs
laced into free holes
and glued down

front   back

finishing inside hot pants

Fig. 179

Plate 53

SUEDE JACKET WITH MACHINE APPLIQUE

Since other forms of appliqué were introduced in preceding projects, you'll have no trouble working with the type used here.

MATERIALS

> Two 18-foot reversible suede skins (used here: red)
> Suede scraps (used here: navy blue)
> Leather scraps (used here: white)
> Thread
> Tissue paper
> Scissors
> Leather glue
> Zipper
> Sewing machine

The jacket was cut from Vogue's pattern #8047. Because it is a blouse pattern, add ½-inch on each seam line, or it will be too tight. Include this ½-inch extra on the sleeve seams also. Construct the jacket according to pattern directions using tissue paper on all inside seams. Glue all the seams open.

My appliqué design was adapted from an American Indian design I found in a book. The finished product barely resembles the original.

Cut your appliqué design, then place all pieces on the suede without pasting. Notice how my design spills over onto the front of the jacket. The circular pieces were placed one on top of the other (plate 54). Tack the suede in place with glue (plate 55). If you use leather that stretches easily, it would be advisable to glue them down firmly. Some leathers, like cabretta, stretch when sewn, especially when sewing around curves.

To machine appliqué, you must sew around each piece, as close to the edge as possible. You can use thread that matches each color of suede or, as was done here, you can use a color that contrasts with some of the pieces. Use tissue paper under the wrong side of your jacket when sewing to help it move through the machine smoothly. If you use large pieces of paper on the right side, they will hide your stitches. Instead, use short, ½-inch wide strips of brown paper (plate 56). Small pieces can be placed more easily around the edges and allow you to see what you're doing.

Plate 54

Plate 55

Plate 56

HOOKED LEATHER AND SUEDE JACKET

Since the sweater will not show after you have finished, purchase the most inexpensive one you can find or use an old baggy or slightly ripped one. Be sure that it's a loose knit and larger than your normal size.

You can limit yourself to one color or several colors in the same value or use a wide variety of contrasting colors. They can be hooked in strips, in designs or haphazardly.

MATERIALS

> Leather and suede scrap strips, 4 to 6-inches long and ¼ to ¾-inches wide
> Loosely knit sweater
> Medium crochet hook

To make this jacket, at least 2 large hides will be needed. Cut strips ¼ to ¾-inches wide, then cut again into 4 to 6-inches long for hooking.

Start hooking anywhere. Double one strip. Loop it around the thread. Pull the loose ends of the thong through the loop created when you doubled it (fig. 180). Use the crochet hook to make this process easier. Continue until the entire sweater is hooked. When you're done you'll have a thick, hairy-looking, wooly-booly jacket which will make you look like a teddy bear (fig. 181).

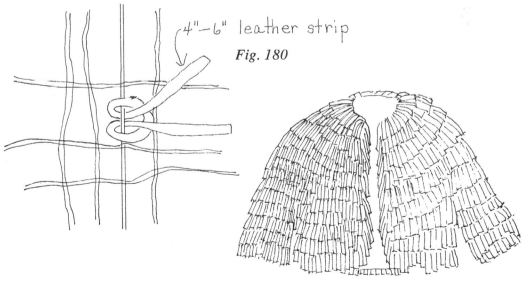

4"–6" leather strip

Fig. 180

Fig. 181

SUEDE HAT

Materials

Split suede cowhide or large scraps (used here; forest green)
Lightweight suede to line the hat brim
Suede scrap (used here; black)
Embroidery thread in several colors
Revolving punch
Awl
Leather glue
Scissors
Harness needle
Pellon
Small sheet brown paper
String

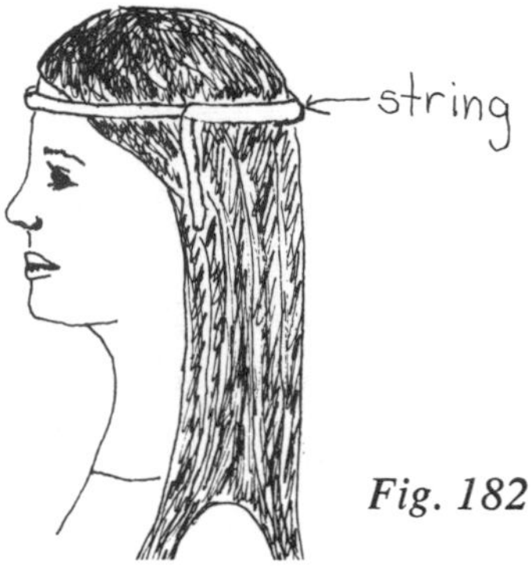

Fig. 182

Making A Hat Pattern

There are hat patterns you can buy commercially. However, you can easily make your own. Measure around your head with a piece of string (fig. 182). Then lay the string on the paper in a circle. Draw around it on the inside. This is the top section of the crown. Draw another circle 3-inches outside this one for the brim (fig. 183). Cut the sides of the crown by making a rectangular shape 4-inches wide, and as long as your head measurement plus 2 inches, for the overlapping seam (fig. 184). The midsection for my hat was done in two pieces because I didn't have a large enough scrap to make it in one piece. Cut a duplicate of the hat brim from the lightweight suede making the outer dimensions slightly larger. You can use a contrasting color or try to match the color of your cowhide. Set this piece aside.

Working with the midsection first, paste Pellon onto the wrong side. Using the second largest hole in the punch, make a single row of holes through each short side of the rectangle; (this will be the side seam). Using thongs of black suede in a running stitch pattern, lace the two overlapped sides together. Now, punch holes around the bottom of the midsection spacing them ½-inch apart (plate 57). Punch holes ½-inch apart around the inside of the brim also. Before attaching the top you must punch all the holes for the decorations you're going to add. Once the top is on, it will be impossible to reach certain areas. Lace the midsection to the brim with the stitch illustrated (fig. 185). Lace away from you, holding the brim of the hat in your left hand for best results (plate 58).

To get a woven effect, punch holes at random distances from each other, and not, necessarily, in a straight line on the mid-section. But whatever the direction you choose to go, *make parallel lines* of holes close to each other (fig. 186). Weave in and out with long black thongs. Finish on the wrong side and glue the ends down.

Use 3/16-inch wide thongs for knotting, thin thongs are easier to knot. Knot as described in the project for the pasted appliqué belt, using the second largest hole on your punch. Glue all loose ends to the inside of the hat.

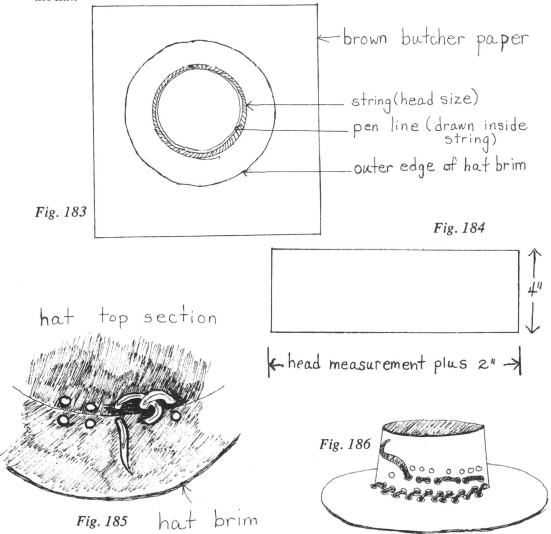

brown butcher paper

string (head size)
pen line (drawn inside string)
outer edge of hat brim

Fig. 183

Fig. 184

4"

head measurement plus 2"

hat top section

Fig. 186

Fig. 185 hat brim

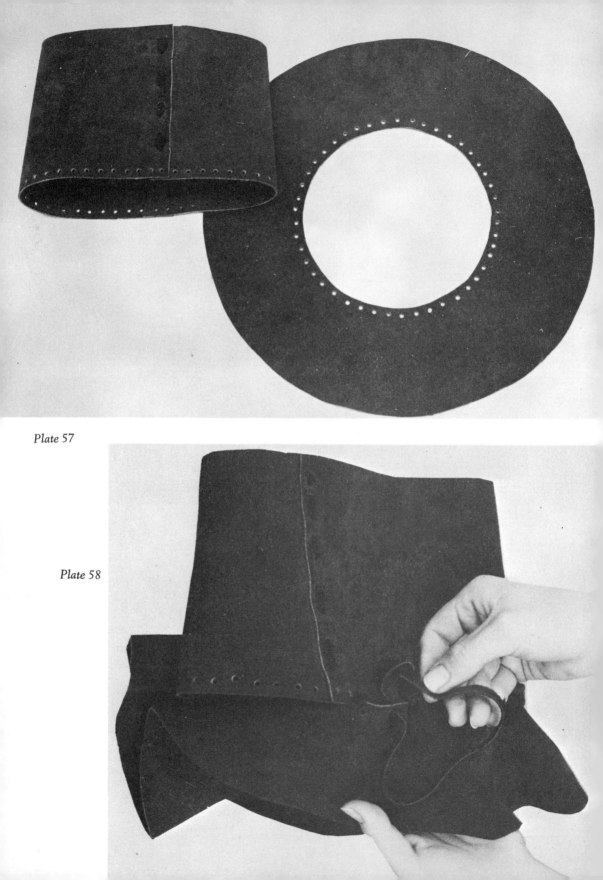

Plate 57

Plate 58

EMBROIDERY STITCHES

There are 5 different embroidery stitches used. To make French knots, start by punching 2 very small holes very close to each other for each knot (or make these holes with an awl). With doubled thread, sew from the wrong side of the hat to the right side. Wrap the thread tightly 5 times around the needle point and as close as possible to the hole you just came through (fig. 187). Pulling tightly on the long end of your thread, push the needle through the hole nearest to the hole you first came through. Hold the knot tightly as close to the hole as possible until you have pulled all the thread through and secured the French knot on the wrong side with a double knot.

Begin the chain stitch by punching a single row of holes. To start, thread through the first hole. Loop it around the second hole, thread down through the first hole again being careful not to catch the beginning of your thread. Come up through the second hole catching the loop as you do so. Repeat until you run out of holes (fig. 188).

The back stitch is begun by making either rows or clusters of holes. When working on clusters, sew *up* one hole and *down* another at random. For single rows, sew *up* the first hole, *down* the second, *up* the third and back *down* the second. Continue to the last hole (fig. 189).

For the stem stitch, you again need a single row of holes. Sew *up* the first hole, *down* the third, *up* the second and *down* the fourth (fig. 190).

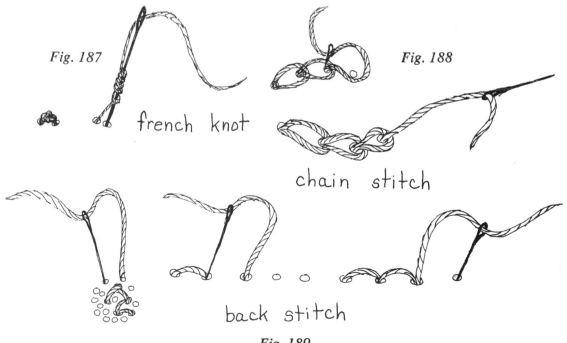

Fig. 187

french knot

Fig. 188

chain stitch

back stitch

Fig. 189

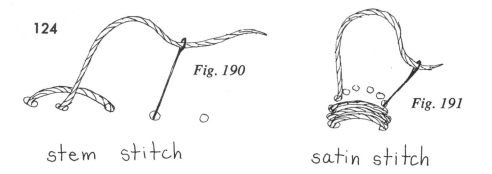

Fig. 190

Fig. 191

stem stitch   satin stitch

The last stitch used is the satin stitch. Because it's impossible to get the holes very close to each other it would be better to call this the open satin stitch. It's more often used to make solid areas. To begin, punch small holes around the perimeter of the shape you want filled in (fig. 191). Stitch across to opposite holes until the area is filled in.

You'll sometimes have to fold the midsection of the hat in upon itself to make many of your holes when using the punch because it won't reach certain areas otherwise.

Once all stitching and decoration is finished on the hat brim, glue the lightweight suede brim to the underside. This will cover the underside of the stitching. Be careful that the glue does not seep through any holes onto the right side. Trim the edges if necessary.

LACING THE SECTIONS

Punch holes using the second largest hole on the punch, along the top edge of the midsection ½-inch apart in the following way: Punch only one hole in the top circle. Start lacing, using this one hole. Line up and punch the second hole. Lace, using this hole. Continue punching and lacing *one hole at a time* holding the hat brim in your right hand this time. As you lace, pull the top circle tightly out towards the edge. By doing this, an excess may develop along the unlaced edge (fig. 192). Trim this off, a little at a time, as you go before punching each successive hole. Working this way, you'll end up with a fairly tight-fitting crown (plate 59).

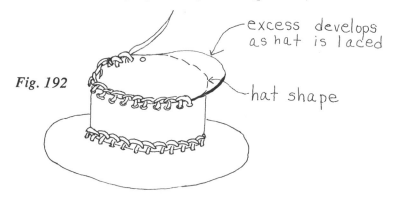

excess develops as hat is laced

Fig. 192

hat shape

Plate 59

LEATHER SHOULDER BAG

You can make a paper pattern for your shoulder bag or, if you prefer you can measure directly on the leather, always marking on the wrong side.

MATERIALS

 Lightweight leather skin (used here: cabretta)
 Suede skin (used here: lamb)
 Pellon
 Scissors
 Leather glue
 Straightedge
 Thread
 Tissue paper
 Heavy brown paper strips
 Acrylic paints
 1 tube gel, medium to keep paints moist
 3-ounce bottle polymer, medium to make paints transparent
 Brushes
 Water

CUTTING A SHOULDER BAG

Either way, cut 5 leather pieces. Cut 1 front piece 9 x 12-inches. Mark the center bottom and draw a line, 2-inches from, and parallel to, the top edge (fig. 193). Cut 1 back piece 9 x 20-inches. Mark the center bottom. Draw a line 10-inches up from the bottom and parallel to it (fig. 194). Cut 1 single piece for the side and bottom, measuring 3 x 24 inches. Draw a line across the center of this piece (fig. 195). Cut 2 shoulder pieces 3 inches x 32-inches (fig. 196). Round off all the corners on the front and back pieces. For all seams, allow ½-inch unless otherwise indicated.

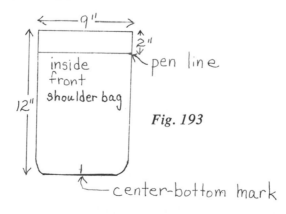

Fig. 193

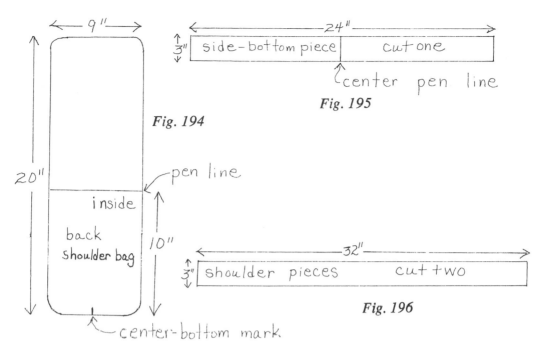

←— 9" —→

Fig. 194

20"

inside

back
shoulder bag

10"

—pen line

center-bottom mark

←————————————— 24" —————————————→

↑3"↓ | side-bottom piece | cut one

center pen line

Fig. 195

←——————————————— 32" ———————————————→

↑3"↓ | shoulder pieces | cut two

Fig. 196

REINFORCING AND SEWING

Cut one piece of Pellon 3 x 32-inches. Paste this to the wrong side of one shoulder piece. Sew the short ends of this piece to the short ends of the bottom-and-side piece, right sides together (plate 60). Use tissue paper at all times, on top of and under the leather, when sewing. Paste the seam down toward the bottom of the bag. Line up the center marks of the front and the bottom-and-side piece, right sides together. Sew from these center marks, easing and fitting the straight edge around the curve. Continue up to the 2-inch line at the top of the bag (plate 61). Returning to the center mark, sew up the other side front. Match the center marks of the back piece to the opposite edge of the bottom-and-side piece the same way. Sew up to the 10-inch line.

Plate 60

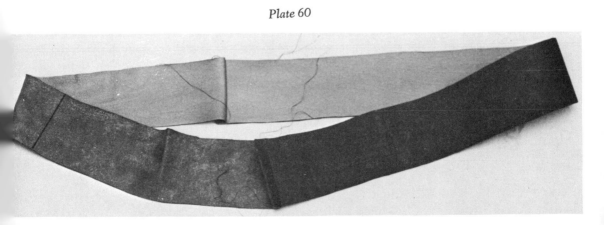

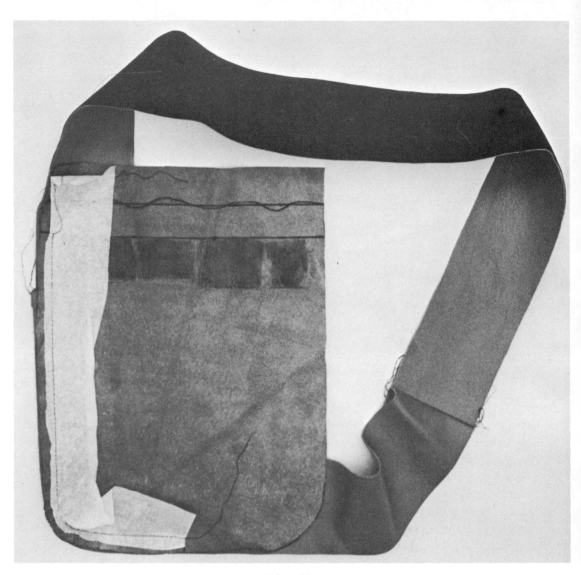

Plate 61

You now have the shell of the bag completed. Cut a piece of Pellon 2 x 8½ inches. Paste it below the 2 inch line on the inside of the front piece. Fold this front edge down to the inside of your bag. Fold the shoulder piece edges in ½-inch and glue (plate 62). This will leave you with a 2-inch span across the shoulder strap.

With the remaining loose shoulder piece, back the upper shoulder piece. Fold the edges of this piece in, matching the edges to the upper piece. Be sure they do not stick out beyond your top piece. When you're sure that it will fit, glue the edges in and pin it to the top piece. Stitch from the inside of the bag, with this inside shoulder piece facing you. Use brown paper strips when sewing, lining up paper and leather edges.

With a hidden stitch, hand sew the front inside edge to the inside shoulder piece where the two meet (figs. 197 and 198).

Fold in the free edges of the back piece ½-inch all around, (easing around the corners) and glue it down (plate 63).

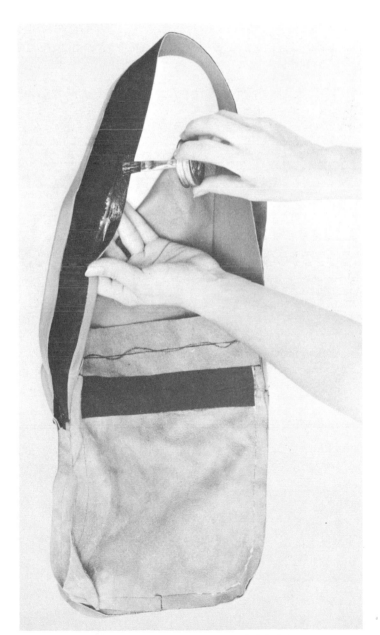

Plate 62

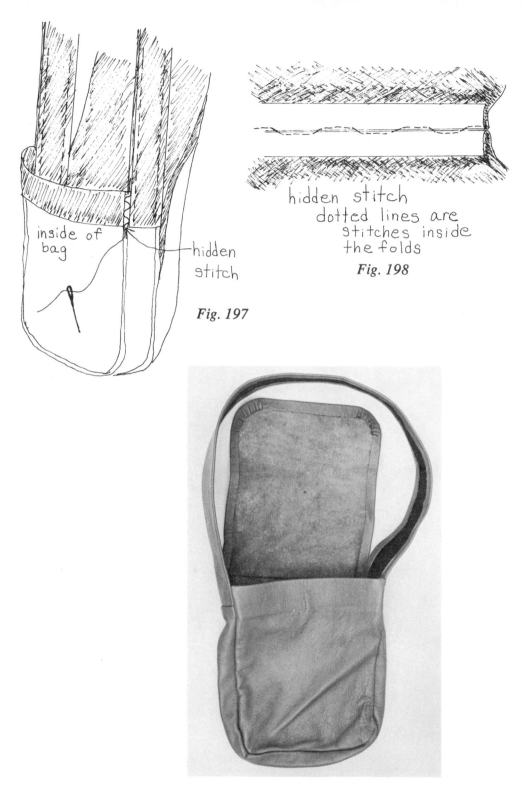

inside of bag

hidden stitch

Fig. 197

hidden stitch
dotted lines are
stitches inside
the folds

Fig. 198

Plate 63

LINING THE BAG

For the lining, cut 3 pieces of suede; 1 front, 1 back and 1 bottom-and-side piece. Cut these pieces ⅛-inch smaller than the bag on all edges.

Mark the centers of these pieces the same way you marked the leather pieces. Mark the front top line 2-inches from the top edge. Mark the back piece 9½-inches from the bottom edge. Sew these pieces together with ½-inch seams, the same way you joined the leather pieces.

Try the lining in the bag for fit. Fold the top lining edge down to within ¼ inch of the top edge of the leather. Keep the fold of the lining in place with pins on the edge. *Do not pin it to the leather*. Once pinned, take the lining out. Sew it down along the front side edges. Then sew the back flap edges about 3-inches down from the fold line with an edge stitch (fig. 199).

Fit the lining back into the bag. Pin the lining to the leather along the side and front top edges. Stitch with the suede facing you from the back side seam to the other back side seam. Use brown paper under the leather when sewing.

Fold the flap lining edge in and pin to within ⅛-inch of the leather's edge. If you find a lot of excess suede when you're folding it in, trim it off as you go, especially around the corners. Sew as close to the edge as possible (plate 64).

This bag is very soft. For more strength you can paste Pellon to all leather pieces before sewing. To help retain its shape add lightweight cardboard but slightly smaller than the front, back, side and bottom pieces. Tack these in place with glue before lining. Do not use cardboard on the flap of the bag.

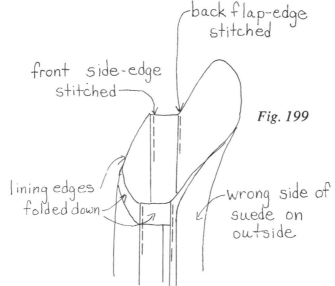

back flap-edge stitched

front side-edge stitched

Fig. 199

lining edges folded down

wrong side of suede on outside

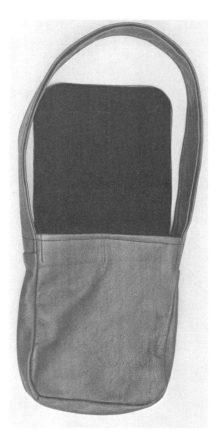

Plate 65

Plate 64

Painting On The Bag

The best paints to use on leather are acrylics which dry very quickly. If you've never used them, experiment on a scrap before painting directly on your shoulder bag. Acrylics come in a wide range of colors. If you prefer, you can buy the exact colors you want without the bother of mixing. Wash all your brushes with soap and water when you're finished painting. If you're going to mix your own colors and thus keep your paints to a minimum, you'll need cadmium yellow light, cadmium red medium, blue (either permanent blue or Prussian blue), white, and black. When mixing your colors use the gel medium to keep them moist. To obtain transparent glazes mix the polymer medium with your paints. The more you use, the more transparent your colors will be. You can mix colors by applying one transparent glaze over another. If you do make a mistake, wipe it off *immediately* with a damp sponge or wet paper towel. Plate 65 shows a finished bag with a painted decoration on the flap.

TOOLING LEATHER

Tooling is the process of decorating leather by permanently impressing a design into it. The methods described here are the mere basics necessary to get you started. There are many books in the field which explain tooling in much more detail.

Personally, tooling is not the medium I would choose because I prefer to work as though I'm baking a cake—a little bit of this, a little bit of that, and voila—a work of art. For me, it's more satisfying to put things together as in a college than to separate them as in a drawing. Both methods are simply ways of breaking up the space to make it more interesting.

If you like working as though you were drawing, you'll enjoy the art of tooling. There are many more tools available than those I have chosen. When you buy stamping tools, try to visualize the designs you can make with each one alone or several in combination.

Suede or chrome-tanned cowhide will not retain a stamped impression. Vegetable-tanned cowhide is the best leather to use for all types of tooling. It is a smooth-surfaced, natural-colored, stiff leather. The process that prepares cowhide for tooling and some of the finishing methods will help soften it (so will wearing it). Cowhide comes in various thicknesses called ounces. One-ounce leather is 1/64-inch thick; 8-ounce is 8/64-inch thick (or ⅛-inch). You can tool almost any thickness if you are careful that you don't punch through the leather unintentionally.

Five different tooling methods will be described: embossing, outline tooling, flat modeling, incising and stamping.

TRACING A DESIGN

When I can't decide on a design, or if I feel that what I have in mind must be more definite before I start to work on the piece, itself, I start sketching. I make several actual-size drawings of the shape to be worked on so that if I do come up with something I really like, it won't be grossly out of proportion. I make many sketches within these shapes until I hit on a design I really want to use. Once the design is decided, I usually work directly on the leather rather than transferring the design. Naturally, it will not be reproduced exactly, when working this way. I find that this difference is negligible in the final product and often more delightful than the original sketch.

If you do have a design which you want to transfer exactly, place tracing paper over it and simply copy. Place this copy over your damp leather piece and fasten it with masking tape (applied to the wrong side of the leather, only). Using the thin, pointed end of a spoon and tracer modeling tool, go over the lines, applying pressure as you do so. Wherever this is done an indentation will be left. Pencils, pens or other marking tools should not be used on the right side of the leather because they won't wash off (fig. 200).

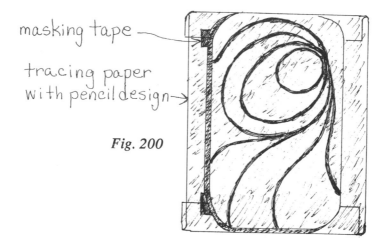

masking tape

tracing paper
with pencil design→

Fig. 200

EMBOSSED LEATHER BELT BUCKLE

MATERIALS

8 or 9-ounce vegetable-tanned cowhide (tooling leather)
Crome-tanned thong (strong thread or other strong leather strip can be
   substituted)
Leather knife (skiving knife)
Spoon and tracer modeling tool or ball end modeling tool
Revolving punch
Leather glue
Sandpaper (fine grain)
Newspaper scrap
Sponge
India inks

Decide the shape you want for the buckle and cut 2 of them with your
leather knife. Cut 2 strips 1-inch wide and 1-inch longer than the height
of the buckle (fig. 201).

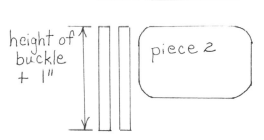

Fig. 201

CASING THE LEATHER

Using a mild soap, scrub all the pieces with a soft bristle brush. Wash the
soap off thoroughly and put the pieces in clean water to soak for a few
minutes. Besides removing the dirt, this process causes the fibers to swell
making the leather soft and pliable. This is called casing the leather.

Take them out of the water and let them dry. Be careful how you
handle the leather now as almost anything will leave an impression or a mar.
Dry them gently with a towel.

To work the leather, wait until it is just starting to return to its natural color. If water squeezes out of it when you press it, it's still too wet and won't hold a deep impression. Let it dry awhile longer. If it becomes too dry while you're working on it, dampen it with a clean sponge.

EMBOSSING

When it's ready to work, hold the leather in your hand wrong side up (plate 66). To emboss, you must push the surface out from the back. The ball end modeler is perfect for this, but embossing can be done with the wide curved end of the spoon and tracer modeling tool as well. As this tool is more versatile than the ball end modeler, you may choose to invest in the spoon and tracer only. Actually any household tool with a small, rounded end would do as well. While pressing into the area you want raised, rub back and forth and in circles. When you think you've raised it enough, turn it over and place it on a hard, flat surface. With the spoon end of the tool, press flat the areas around the embossing (plate 67).

If you now decide that your design is not raised enough, turn it over and repeat the process. Do this as many times as necessary to get the height you want. When you're satisfied, let the piece dry thoroughly. Fill the hole with crumpled newspaper. Use glue to keep the paper in place, so that the back surface is flat (plate 68).

Plate 66

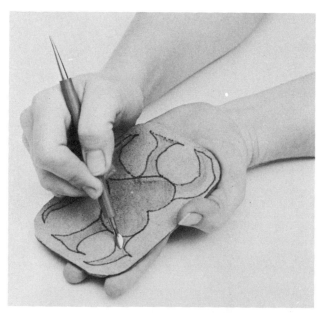

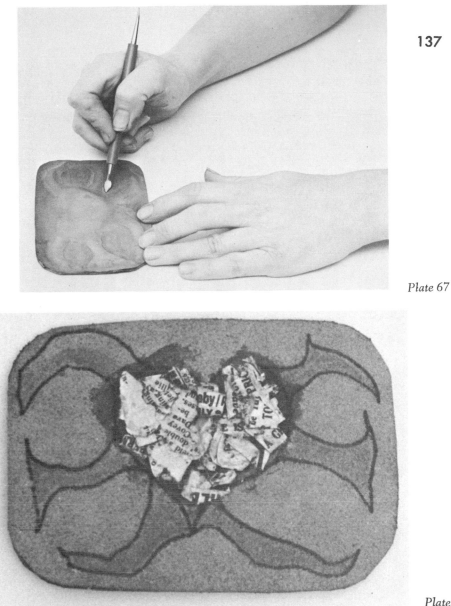

Plate 67

Plate 68

Preparing the Buckle Backing

The remaining duplicate shape is the backing for the buckle. Make 2 parallel slits at both ends of this shape (fig. 202). Thin down the ends of the 2 straps by cutting away the excess from the wrong side or by sanding it down. Slip these ends through the slits so that you have 2 loops on the right side of the buckle backing (fig. 203). One loop is necessary to attach the belt; the other to hold the loose end of the belt in place. Glue the edges you've just slipped through the slits, to the inside of the backing piece.

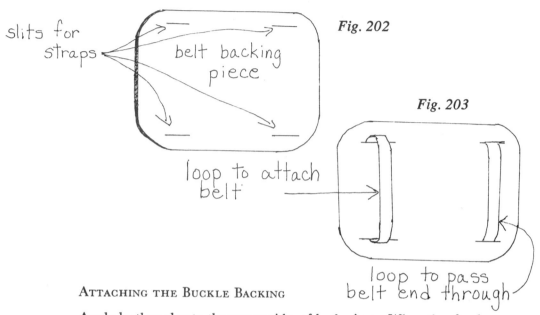

slits for straps

belt backing piece

Fig. 202

Fig. 203

loop to attach belt

loop to pass belt end through

Attaching the Buckle Backing

Apply leather glue to the wrong sides of both pieces. When the glue becomes tacky, press them together. Pressure will be necessary to assure proper bonding; but because this piece is raised it should not be put under heavy weights. Instead, roll up some paper towels and place them on the right side of the buckle to protect this surface, then clip the bonded pieces together around the edges using spring type clothespins. When the glue has dried, you may notice that the back edges show in some spots. Use the leather knife to carefully cut these edges even with the front. Sand the edges smooth, rubbing in one direction.

Decorating With India Inks

Apply India inks with a brush according to your design. Be sure to color the edges as well. When the inks are thoroughly dry, apply a neutral paste wax to any areas you have colored. Rub in well.

Attaching A Belt

When cutting a strap of leather for a belt, take into account the size of the pants loops they must pass through. Cut the strap that width or smaller and about 8-inches longer than the waist size. Fold one end around one of the loops on the back of the belt buckle and punch 2 parallel holes through both thicknesses. Using a thong of chrome-tanned cowhide, knot one end, pass the unknotted end through one set of holes, around and through the remaining set of holes and knot again. Cut off the excess (fig. 204).

Do any coloring or designing on the belt itself before you attach it to the buckle (plate 69).

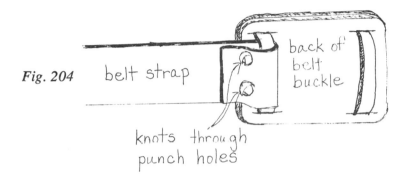

Fig. 204   belt strap   back of' belt buckle

knots through punch holes

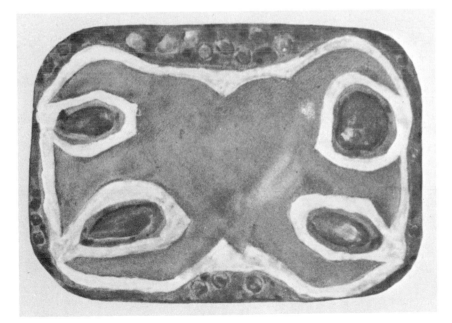

Plate 69

TOOLED KEY TAB

MATERIALS

> Vegetable-tanned cowhide
> Spoon and tracer modeling tool
> Revolving punch
> Leather glue
> 7 leather or suede thongs, each 6-inches long
> Acrylic paints
> Polymer medium
> Leather dyes (used here: antique mahogany and purple)
> Brushes
> Cotton swabs
> Paper towels
> Leather lacquer spray

> Cut 2 pieces the same size for the front and back of the key tab.
> Case the leather as described for the belt buckle.
> Punch 6 or 7 holes along the bottom edge of one piece.

OUTLINE TOOLING

For outline tooling use the tracer end of the modeling tool. While applying pressure, simply draw lines as you would with a pencil (plate 70).

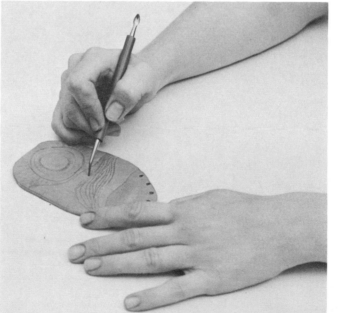

Plate 70

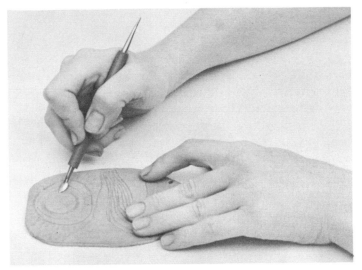

Plate 71

Flat Modeling

For flat modeling use the spoon end of the modeling tool to depress areas on the right side of the leather. Press down firmly, going over the same area many times (plate 71).

Textures can be made by using the edge of the same end when depressing the leather. These marks can be grouped close to each other or spread out.

One or both sides of the leather can be tooled as desired.

Painting

Apply acrylic paints and the purple dye with brushes. Use a cotton swab (as explained in the project for the bracelet) to apply antique dye. Set aside until thoroughly dry.

Finishing

Glue both pieces back to back. Punch holes through the second piece. Bond together firmly by placing heavy weights on top of them until they dry.

Once dry, trim any excess. Sand the edges smooth. Apply dye to the edges. Coat with leather lacquer or polymer medium for a final protective finish.

Knot each thong at one end and make a point at the other end. Pull one thong through each hole. Attach a key by pushing a pointed end through the hole in the key and knot the thong again to keep it in place (plate 72).

See the projects for the shoulder bag, picture frame and the suede painting; for details on using acrylics.

When working with dyes, follow the manufacturer's directions. Most dyes are simply flowed and rubbed in while the excess is wiped off.

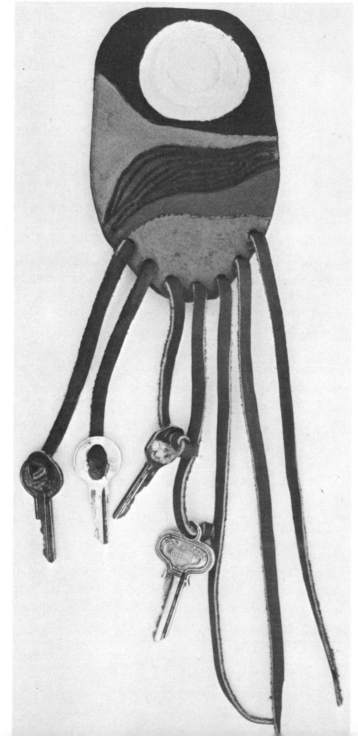

Plate 72

INCISED AND STAMPED BRACELET

MATERIALS

    Vegetable-tanned cowhide
    Swivel knife
    Leather knife
    Stamping tools (used here: small star, small circle, camouflage tool)
    Hard work-board
    Mallet
    Revolving punch
    2 chrome-tanned thongs, 6-inches long
    Antique mahogany leather dye
    Gold leaf
    Cotton swabs
    Leather lacquer spray

For a bracelet, only 1 piece will be needed. Cut it the shape you wish. Try it on your wrist to be sure that it will fit. Case the leather as described for the belt buckle.

INCISING

The swivel knife does not cut away any leather. Instead, as it carves the surface, it pushes the leather down and to either side of the knife thus compacting the leather into V-grooved lines. Hold the knife at a 45° angle with the lifted corner of the blade towards you. Loop your index finger over the curved bar at the top; rest your pinky on the leather to help guide your strokes. Use your other fingers to grasp the handle above the blade. Keeping the blade at a 45° angle pull it toward you, twirling the handle between your fingers as you go to create curved cuts. Practice this on a scrap before working on your final piece. With very little pressure it should carve the surface of the leather like butter (plate 73).

STAMPING

When you place the stamping tool on the leather, you'll notice that the working end does not sit flat unless the tool is held at an angle. Once it is positioned properly tap the tool sharply with the mallet. Don't hit it too hard, it's possible to cut all the way through the leather (plate 74). Most tooling only cuts about halfway through. Do all stamping with a hard board under the leather. When all the stamping and incising is done let the piece dry thoroughly.

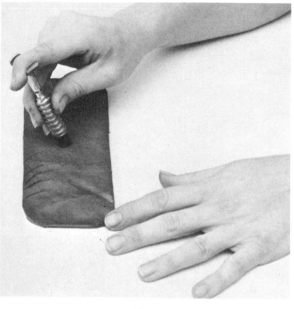

Plate 73

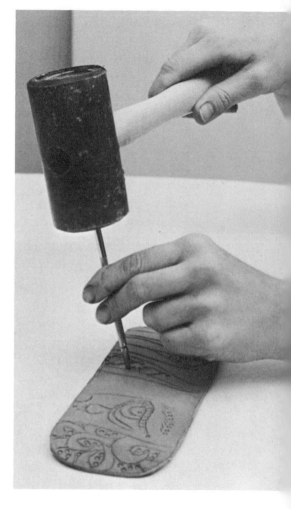

Plate 74

APPLYING ANTIQUE DYES

Apply the antique finish heavily with a cotton swab or piece of cardboard, and be sure to get into all the little crevices. Set it aside for a little while and then scrape off the excess carefully. If you use cardboard, you can return this excess to the jar. Don't press too hard with the cardboard; you may scratch the leather. Take off the rest of the excess with a soft cloth but don't pull the dye out of the crevices. Let the piece dry. Finish by rubbing it with a soft cloth or soft paper towels until no more dye comes off.

GOLD LEAFING

The gold leaf I used is the kind that comes in small sheets (it looks as though it was painted on a piece of cellophane). Place this sheet on the leather with the shiny side facing you and rub over the area with a hard rounded instrument (I used the end of a paintbrush) to transfer the gold to the leather. Spray lacquer on the entire piece or the gold will rub off (plate 75).

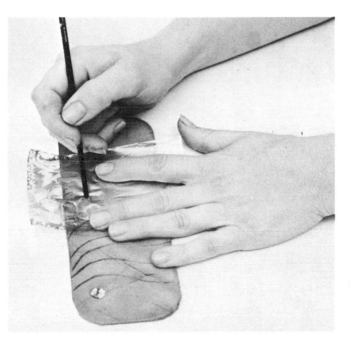

Plate 75

MAKING A SIMPLE CLOSING

Punch 4 holes in the ends of the bracelet; placing 2 holes at each end facing each other. Knot one end of each thong. Pass each unknotted end through a hole (plate 76). Then pass the thongs through the holes opposite them (on the other end). Fit the bracelet to your wrist and knot tightly to keep it in place. All knots will show on the right side. Cut off the excess thong and slip the bracelet off your wrist (plates 77 and 78).

If you would like to make an adjustable bracelet that you can tighten, loop one long thong through all 4 holes so that it can be pulled tight and tied (fig. 205).

Plate 76

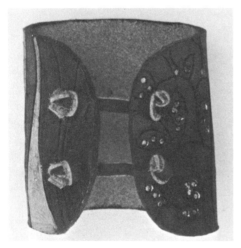

Plate 77

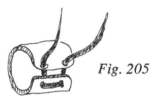

Fig. 205

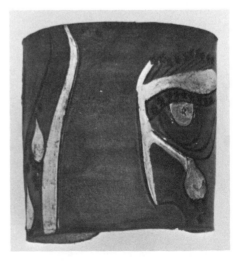

Plate 78

SANDALS

Materials

Heavy paper (for pattern)
 8-ounce leather (vegetable tanned and enough to cut 4 foot shapes)
 6-ounce strap leather
 Leather knife
 Glue
 Roughing tool or stiff wire brush
 Awl
 Waxed thread (at least 5-ply)
 Sandpaper (fine grain)
 Spoon and tracer modeling tool
 Sponge rubber (optional, for heel padding, ¼ or ½-inch thick)
 Beeswax (for setting edges)
 Large-eyed needle

Place your right foot on a piece of heavy paper and trace around it (fig. 206). Enlarge this tracing ⅛-inch all around smoothing out the lines as you do so (fig. 207).

Make two tracings of this pattern on the 8-ounce leather. Flip this pattern over and make two more. This will give you two pieces for the right foot and two for the left (fig. 208). Using the leather knife, cut out the four pieces.

Use 1-inch wide strips of heavy paper to find the length of the toe straps needed and a ½-inch wide strip for the heel strap. Place these strips around your foot where the leather straps are to be (fig. 209). Add 1-inch on each strap end for the portion that is to be connected to the rest of the sandal (fig. 210). Cut 4 straps 1-inch wide and 2 straps ½-inch wide from the 6-ounce leather according to the measurements you just made with the paper strips. Remember you can place your straps anywhere you like and use as many as you like.

Fig. 206

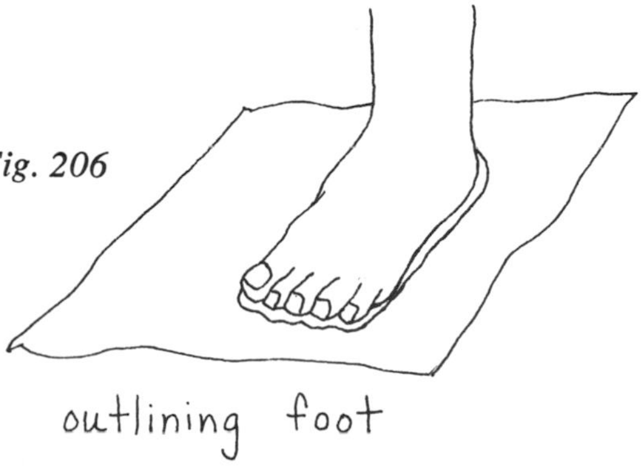

outlining foot

foot tracing enlarged ⅛ "
all around

Fig. 207

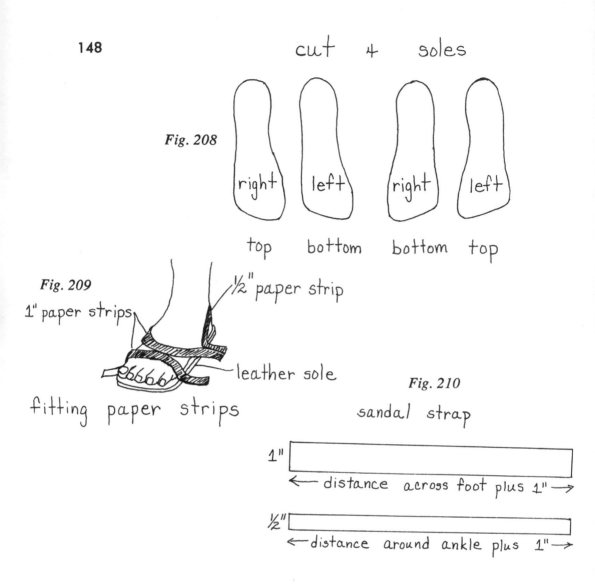

cut 4 soles

Fig. 208

right left right left

top bottom bottom top

Fig. 209

1" paper strips

½" paper strip

—leather sole

fitting paper strips

Fig. 210

sandal strap

1"

←— distance across foot plus 1" —→

½"

←— distance around ankle plus 1" —→

FITTING THE STRAPS

Mark the strap positions on one right sole by placing your right foot on it and placing the straps where they are comfortable around your foot. These marks must be at least ¼-inch in from the edge. Cut slots where these marks are (fig. 211). Thin the ends of all the straps by cutting off the excess with a leather knife or a skiver (fig. 212). Put them through the slots and fold them out towards the sandal's edge (fig. 213). Place your foot on the sole and pull the end of each strap until it fits snugly. If necessary, cut off any surplus and thin the strap end again.

Before gluing the straps in place copy their length for the left sandal. Also copy the slots onto the left sandal by placing the right sides of the right and left top soles together (fig. 214). When this is done glue all straps in place.

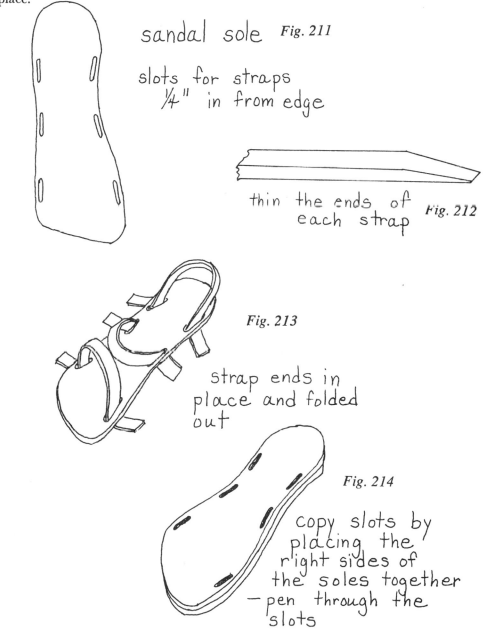

sandal sole *Fig. 211*

slots for straps
¼" in from edge

thin the ends of
each strap *Fig. 212*

Fig. 213

strap ends in
place and folded
out

Fig. 214

copy slots by
placing the
right sides of
the soles together
— pen through the
slots

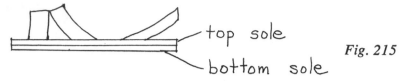

top sole

bottom sole

Fig. 215

GLUING THE SOLES AND PADDING THE HEEL

Rough up the wrong side of each sole piece with a roughing tool or stiff wire brush. Glue the top soles to the bottom soles rough sides together (fig. 215). If you want a cushioned sole, glue a ¼ or ½-inch thick piece of sponge between the soles before gluing them together. Keep this piece of sponge at least ½-inch in from the edge (fig. 216). When glued and dry, trim all edges even with the leather knife.

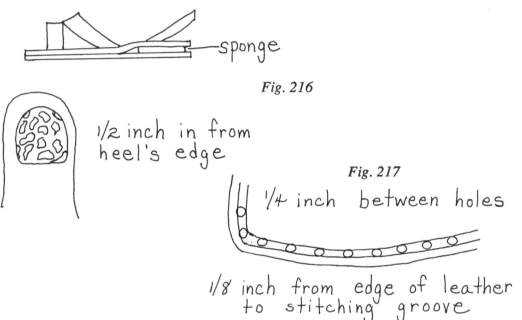

sponge

Fig. 216

½ inch in from heel's edge

Fig. 217

¼ inch between holes

⅛ inch from edge of leather to stitching groove

STITCHING

Cut a groove no more than half the thickness of the leather around the edge of the sole ⅛-inch in from the edge and on both upper and lower soles (see stitching section). Make holes for stitching in this groove ¼-inch apart with the awl (fig. 217). Using these holes sew around the edge using waxed thread and either a running stitch, the backstitch or a sadler's stitch.

FINISHING

Rub the edges with a fine emery cloth in one direction only. Apply beeswax or a neutral paste wax to the edges and use the curved end of the spoon and tracer modeling tool to burnish these edges by rubbing back and forth vigorously. If you're doing it right, the edge will become shiny, smooth, and hard.

You may want to place the straps differently (fig. 218); add heels; either manufactured or cut from the 8-ounce leather (fig. 219); or you may want to tool, paint or dye them.

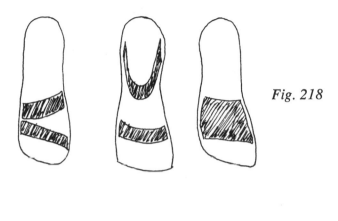

Fig. 218

Fig. 219

heel is made by gluing
2 pieces of 8-ounce
leather together

4. Leather Designs for the Home

PIERCED LAMPSHADE

Technically, piercing means to make a small opening. Although it's stretching this point, you could consider piercing as making any size or shape hole you want.

Use an old lampshade with the covering on, if you plan to use a soft pliable leather. If the old cover is in bad shape remove it from the frame and make a new one. When using a leather that is capable of standing up by itself but also flexible, the covering on the lampshade is not necessary. Be sure the leather can be pierced easily.

MATERIALS

> Lampshade with or without covering
> Medium weight flexible paper, if frame needs recovering
> Ink pad, if recovering
> Glue
> Cotton bias tape, if recovering
> Large leather skin
> Awl

You can make a pattern for your shade by rubbing the edges of the frame on an ink pad and rolling it on paper (fig. 220).

Wind cotton bias tape tightly around all parts of the frame (fig. 221). Glue the ends neatly in place. Cut the new shade cover from a medium weight flexible paper or from a stiff leather; making it the same size as your pattern plus one extra inch on each of the side edges to be overlapped and on the top and bottom edges. Brush glue onto the top and bottom edges and place on the frame. Use clip-on clothespins around both edges to assure bonding.

Cover a paper shade with a piece of soft leather cut 1 inch larger than your pattern on all four sides. Brush vertical strips of glue at 2-inch intervals around the paper cover and place the leather on top, centering it carefully.

Fold the excess leather on the top and bottom edges and glue inside to affix it permanently.

Decide on your pattern for piercing the shade—in strips, swirls, flower designs or haphazardly. You can cluster your holes to produce areas which will let a lot of light through, spread them out, or create thin lines.

Use an awl to pierce the holes.

Piercing depends on light showing through it, to be effective. Other ideas are pierced candle-holders or a chandelier formed over a wire frame (plate 79).

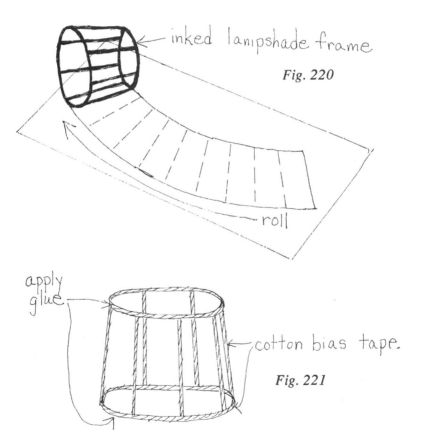

inked lampshade frame

Fig. 220

roll

apply glue

cotton bias tape.

Fig. 221

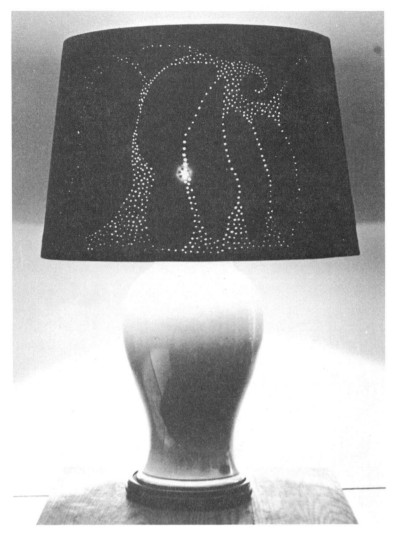

Plate 79

LEATHER TABLETOP

The Parsons table was developed by the Parsons School of Design in the early 1930s. It has certain constant proportions which differentiate it from other tables. The width of the edge of the table and the width of the leg are always equal to each other. Because the legs on my particular Parsons table are square blocks, they are easy to cover with leather.

MATERIALS

    2 skins soft leather (used here: cabretta)
    Preconstructed Parsons table (height 17-inches, top 16 x 16-inches)
       with square legs
    Decorative nails
       190 for nailing legs and top
       500 (assorted) for snake design
    Wood stain (used here: Minwax)
    Leather glue (used here: Franklin liquid hide glue)
    Straightedge
    Awl
    Hammer

Stain the table legs and let them dry.

Cut the top piece of leather so that it overhangs all sides of the table-top by 1-inch (fig. 222). Cut leather for the square legs to fit around the two *outer* sides with 1-inch extra on each side and at the top and bottom.

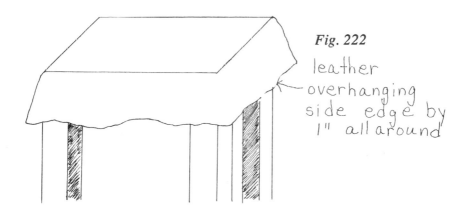

Fig. 222

leather overhanging side edge by 1" all around

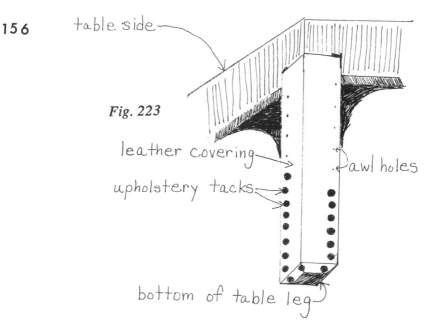

table side

Fig. 223

leather covering

upholstery tacks

awl holes

bottom of table leg

Plate 80

COVERING THE LEGS

Work the legs first. Fold under one edge and place your straightedge along this edge. Starting at the bottom, measure up ½-inch and mark with the awl. Make each succeeding mark 1½-inches apart and mark again with the awl (fig. 223). Hammer a decorative nail into each awl hole (plate 80). Fold under the remaining loose edge, pulling tightly and evenly as you go. Measure, mark and tack as before. Always work the legs from the bottom up.

Turn the table upside-down. Apply glue sparingly to the bottom edges. Fold under the excess leather and nail at 3 corners. Finish all the legs, leaving the top ends of leather free.

COVERING THE TABLETOP

To start on the tabletop, center the leather. Then, find the center of one side and put a nail there. Each succeeding nail should be 2½-inches from the *center* of the last one (figs. 224 and 225). Next work the top edge opposite this one, in the same way, pulling the leather tightly as you work. Work the remaining two top edges.

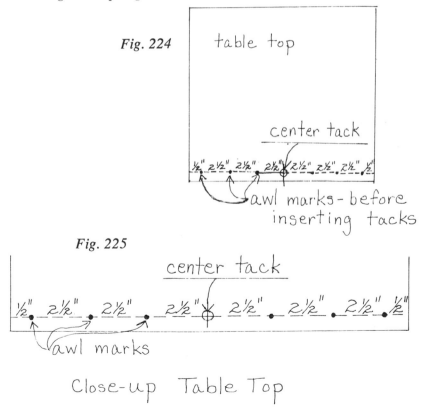

Plate 81

Plate 82

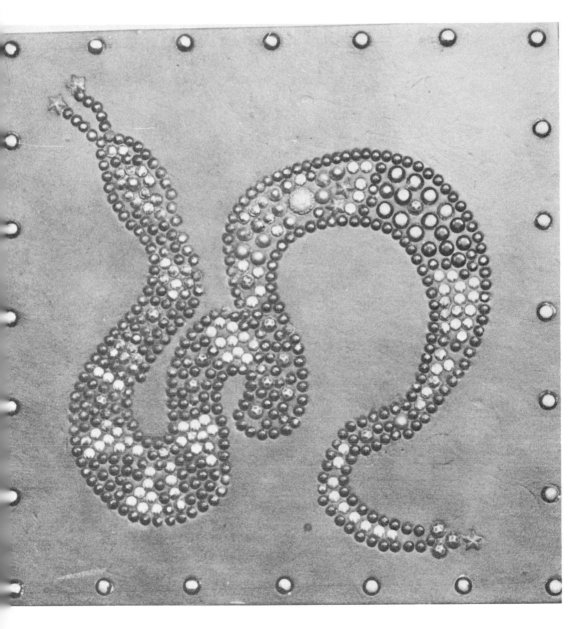

Plate 83

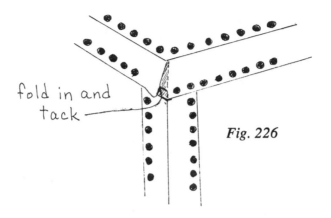

fold in and
tack ———

Fig. 226

COVERING THE SIDES OF THE TOP

The leather hanging loose over the sides of the tabletop can now be tacked. Starting at the center, and working out to the sides, fold under and nail along the bottom edge (plate 81). Work the opposite side. When you're done with both of these, you'll have a flap left on each corner. Work the third side. As you approach the corners, fold the edges in as shown and nail up each corner edge (fig. 226 and plate 82). When you pull the leather tight, be careful you don't pull it out of shape.

Begin the design on the table top by nailing the outline first and then filling in (plate 83).

FOOTSTOOL

MATERIALS

Clear pine, 3-foot plank, 1¼ x 12-inches
Wood contact glue
3 wood poles, 10 feet long x 1½-inch diameter
6 wood screws
Screwdriver
Tools to drill holes for wood screws
Wood stain (used here: brush-on Minwax)
Hammer
Nails
Japanese woodcut knife
Thick piece of cow butt, 16 x 22-inches
Leather knife
24 large decorative nails
Liquid dyes (used here: Rit):
  fuchsia
  rose pink
  purple
Sponge
Black marking pen (waterproof)
Brushes
Clear paste wax

Fig. 227

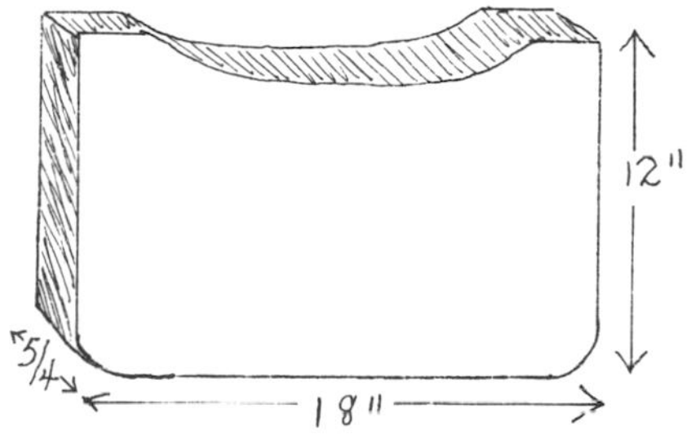

Fig. 228

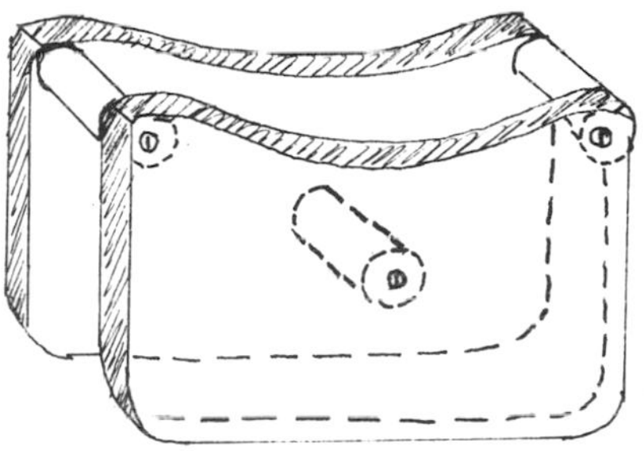

To begin constructing the footstool, cut your 3-foot piece of pine in half. Round the corners with a jigsaw or whittle them round with a Japanese woodcut knife. Cut curves into the top of each piece (fig. 227).

Position the 10-inch dowels level at each upper corner. When doing this, leave the two side pieces standing on a flat surface. Drill your holes carefully or the piece will wrench out of kilter. Drill through the wood sides into the center of the wood poles. Do the middle pole last, once again exerting the same caution as you did when drilling the two corner holes (fig. 228). Insert the screws. For added strength you can dip the screw points in wood glue first. This procedure is not as simple as it sounds. Don't be too concerned if you cannot align the poles properly as the two top corner poles will later be covered with leather. There's a maxim well accepted among artists: "Work with your mistakes."

Using the Japanese woodcut knife, bevel away the edges, cutting in a little deeper along some portions of the edge, to create an antique look. You can further stress the wood by hammering nail holes into it, or just banging on it with a hammer.

Instead of antiquing, you might prefer carving a design into the sides. Your woodcut knife is very good for this.

Stain all the wood, inside the stool and out.

If your piece of leather is exactly 16 x 22-inches, you won't have to cut it down. Mark a 1½-inch border on each long side of the leather and a 2-inch border on each short side. On the longer edges draw a vertical line every 2-inches (fig. 229). Mark ½-inch along the outside edges on both sides of each of the vertical lines (fig. 230). Draw diagonal lines to form points. Cut through these lines with your leather knife removing the wedges (plate 85 and fig. 230). Cut 4 pieces, one out of each corner (plate 84).

With your sponge, wet the leather evenly and thoroughly on both sides and stretch it over the stool. Start at one front corner and fix it in place by hammering a decorative nail into the middle of each flap. Use 3 decorative nails on each end, making sure you catch the wood poles without splitting them (plate 86). Use 2 more decorative nails to cover up the screw hole on each side.

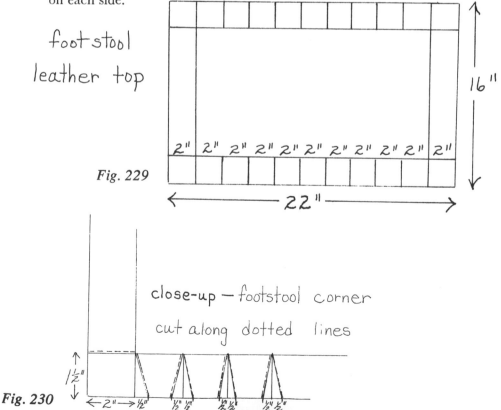

footstool leather top

16"

2" 2" 2" 2" 2" 2" 2" 2" 2" 2" 2"

Fig. 229

22"

close-up — footstool corner

cut along dotted lines

1½"

Fig. 230

←2"→ ½" ½" ½" ½" ½" ½" ½"

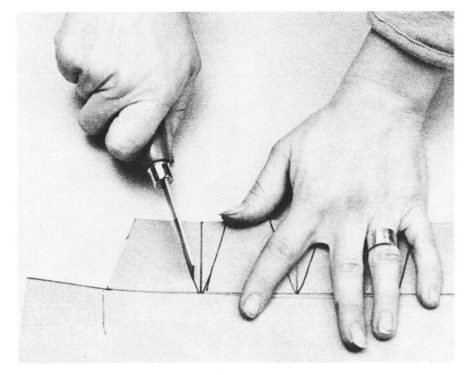

Plate 84

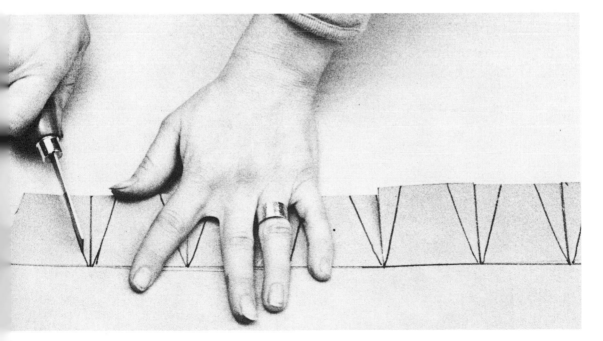

Plate 85

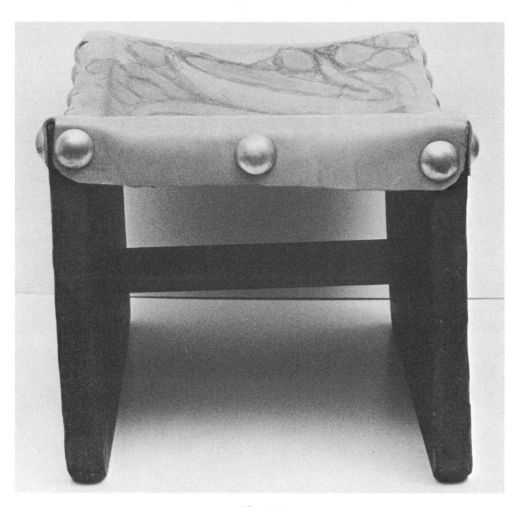

Plate 86

DYEING

Brush on the liquid dyes. For lighter, more delicate colors, first dampen the leather. For darker tones, brush the color on when the leather is dry. When your dyes are dry, sketch around the shapes with your marking pen. Use a clear paste wax to protect the surface.

If you prefer, you can buy leather dyes in various colors and use them to create your design, or you can dye the top all one color.

Neat's-foot oil will darken the leather without dyeing it, and make it more supple (plate 87).

Plate 87

LEATHER PICTURE FRAME

Materials

Reversible cowhide (used here: off-white, leather side)

Acrylic paints: Used here: cadmium red medium, cadmium yellow medium, Prussian blue, burnt sienna, yellow ochre

Acrylic polymer medium, for transparent glazes

Gel medium (keeps paint from drying too quickly)

Brushes

Leather glue, white (used here: Weldwood white glue)

200 upholstery tacks

Scissors

2 pieces ¾-inch pine (used here: 14 x 4-inches)

2 pieces ¾-inch pine (used here: 20 x 4-inches)

2 furring strips, 16-inches long

2 furring strips, 14-inches long

4 flat angle brackets, 3-inch size

Contact wood glue

1 large nail

Smaller nails, for attaching furring strips to back of frame

Picture hooks and wire

The 4 pieces of 4-inch-wide pine will be used to make a frame with a 12 x 16-inch opening. Begin by gluing the four pieces together with wood contact glue. Follow directions on the glue bottle. When bonded firmly together, screw in the flat angle brackets. Nail the furring strips about ¼-inch from the inside opening edge (fig. 231).

Lay your frame face down on the wrong side of the leather. Mark around the inside and outside edges. Cut the outer edge 2-inches wider all around. Cut out the inside leather, leaving a 1-inch border to be folded over and glued to the inside frame edge. Cut the inside border at the corners to the point where the pen marks meet (fig. 232).

Using a scrap piece of cardboard, spread a thick layer of white glue over one front side of your frame (fig. 233). Do the same to the next side and then to each succeeding side until the leather is pasted to the front of the frame only. Glue one outside edge at a time, clipping the excess as each side is glued. Cut the leather at an angle where it is to be folded onto the back of the frame, then glue (fig. 234). Fold and glue the inside leather edges leaving any excess free. When dry, trim this excess even with the inner edge of the back of the frame (fig. 235). Cut small roughly-triangular pieces (with one right angle) and paste into the corners where the wood is still showing. Trim when dry (fig. 236).

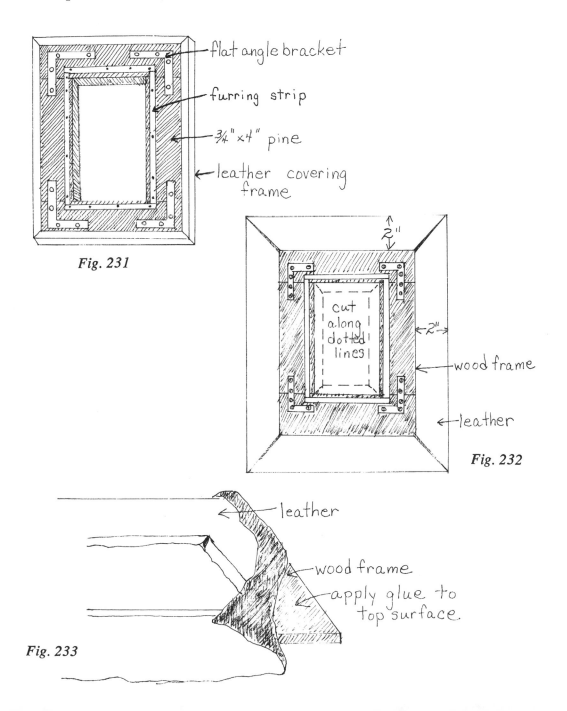

flat angle bracket

furring strip

3/4" x 4" pine

leather covering frame

Fig. 231

cut along dotted lines

←2"→

wood frame

leather

Fig. 232

leather

wood frame

apply glue to top surface.

Fig. 233

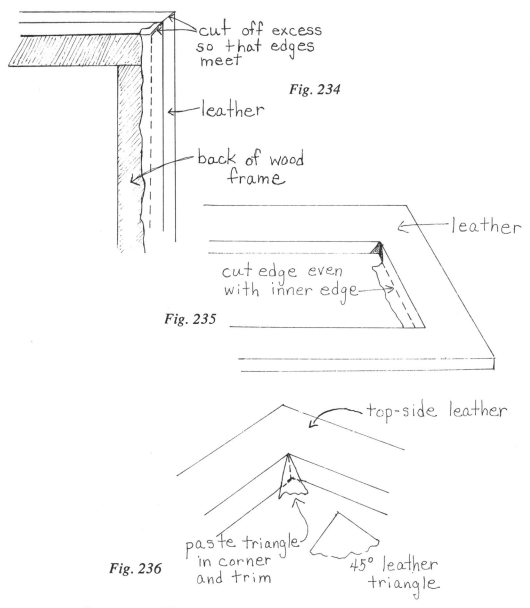

cut off excess so that edges meet

Fig. 234

leather

back of wood frame

leather

cut edge even with inner edge

Fig. 235

top-side leather

paste triangle in corner and trim

Fig. 236

45° leather triangle

DECORATING THE FRAME

Hammer your upholstery tacks in the pattern you want. For this project, I used a large amount of polymer medium with the paints. A yellow transparent glaze was brushed over a red transparent glaze, producing a red-orange. The blue was applied straight from the tube so that it would add a dark contrast.

If you have not used acrylics before, keep a jar of water handy to wash your brushes or wipe away mistakes. The paint dries fast and if allowed to set it may never come off.

This makes an attractive mirror frame, too (plate 88).

Add 1 screw eye on each side of the frame above the middle. Thread picture wire through them.

Plate 88

BOOK JACKET

MATERIALS

> Leather, pliable piece, 2 inches larger all around than your book
> Cardboard
> Leather scraps
> Leather glue
> Scissors
> Straightedge

Cut 2 pieces of cardboard and 1 piece of brown paper the same size as your book cover. Cut your leather piece 2-inches wider than the book's total size, including both covers and the spine. Place the book open in the middle on the wrong side of the leather. Close the book and trace around one cover. Roll it onto its spine and then onto its other cover. This will give you the proper spacing between both covers. Now trace around this cover, too.

Put the book aside and paste the cardboard rectangles within the two outlines on the leather (fig. 237). Cut V's at each corner of the cardboard along the top and bottom edges as shown (fig. 238). Fold and glue the three middle pieces between the V's along the top and bottom edges (fig. 239). Fold down the edge flaps (fig. 240). Apply glue to this area on all four corners and fold in. Leave the inside of the leather free to slip over the book cover (plate 89).

Draw your design on the brown paper rectangle. Cut and trace your shapes onto leather scraps (fig. 241). Fit and glue in place (plate 90).

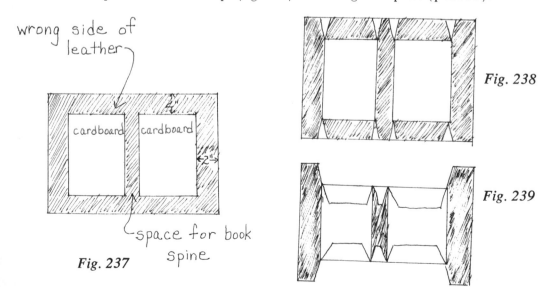

wrong side of leather

cardboard   cardboard

space for book spine

Fig. 237

Fig. 238

Fig. 239

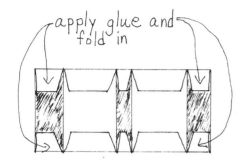

apply glue and fold in

Fig. 240

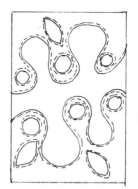

paper rectangle
cut to book
cover size

cut around
drawn design

Fig. 241

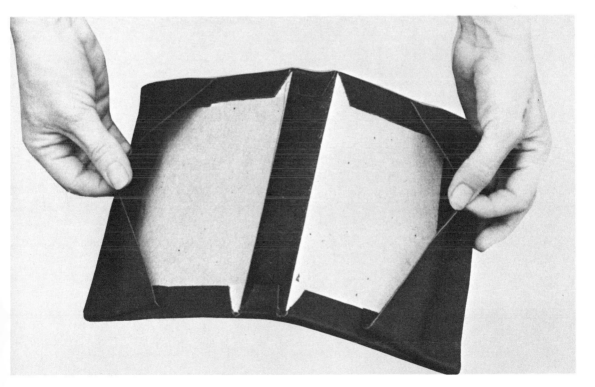

Plate 89

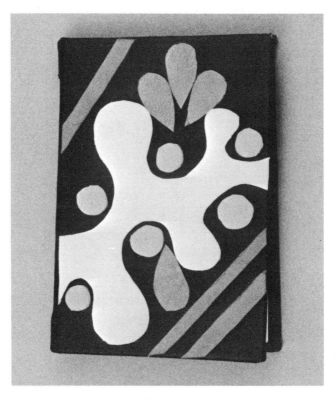

Plate 90

PILLOW

MATERIALS

> 2 large pieces of leather (used here: 17 x 17-inch cabretta)
> Leather scraps, various colors
> Awl
> Sharp embroidery needle, large eye
> Embroidery thread, various colors
> Scissors
> Pellon (same size as cabretta)
> Leather glue
> Pillow stuffing

STUFFING A PILLOW

Before we make the pillow case, let's discuss the pillow. Use an old, still firm bed pillow. Or, for stuffing, use old fabric scraps, a foam rubber form, foam rubber chips, kapok or a combination of foam chips and kapok. If you decide to use kapok or foam chips, make a muslin pillow the same size as your outer pillowcase, to contain them. Kapok is very soft and fluffs up beautifully, but be prepared for a bit of a mess as it is very fine and tends to float all over.

MAKING A PILLOW COVER

Cut 2 pieces of Pellon the same size as the pillow pieces, 17 x 17-inches. Glue them to the inside of the leather pieces. If desired curve the corners. Put these pieces aside.

Use a fairly large leather scrap for the main decorative motif, in this case, an owl. Be sure this shape is at least 1½-inches within the borders of your overall pillow size. For a normal throw pillow, 17-inches square like this one, the motifs should not exceed 14 x 14-inches. Make a paper pattern to see how the owl will look and fit.

The owl feathers are cut from two complementary colors and are rectangles with one rounded end, and where necessary, a curved or slanted top. The beak is a long triangle and each eye three different colors and sizes of circles placed one on top of the other. Smaller "eyebrow" circles were used to add accent. Sometimes a design which uses a lot of sharp-pointed shapes or straight-edged shapes needs to be softened by using rounded shapes for contrast.

Arrange all of these smaller pieces on the large owl form (plate 91). When they're arranged to suit your taste, glue them down. Then glue the entire form to one of the larger leather pieces, to complete one side of the pillow.

Cut any pieces that are going to be outside of the main figure and glue them down, making sure they are at least 1-inch inside the edge of the finished pillow.

While it is still easy to get at the back of this piece, do all of the stitching. See the hat project for directions for making french knots, the chain stitch, the stem stitch and the satin stitch.

Plate 91

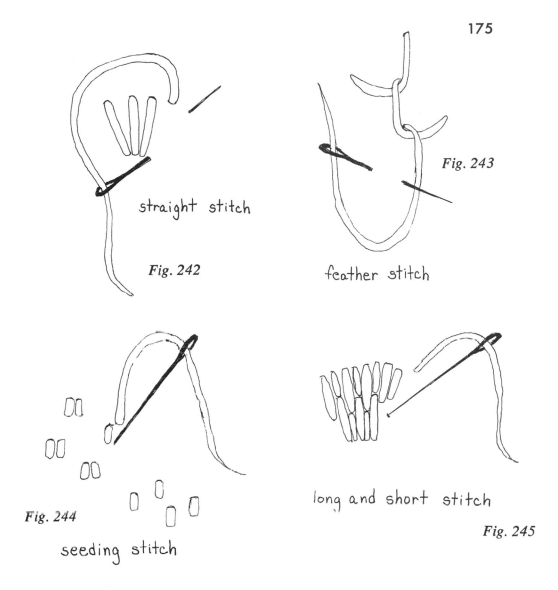

straight stitch

Fig. 242

Fig. 243

feather stitch

Fig. 244

seeding stitch

long and short stitch

Fig. 245

DECORATIVE STITCHES

Some new stitches used were the straight stitch (fig. 242), the long-armed feather stitch (fig. 243), and the seeding stitch (fig. 244).

Although it's not used here, you might want to try the long and short stitch (fig. 245), the bullion stitch (fig. 246), the couching stitch (fig. 247), or the blanket stitch (fig. 248) on a project of your own.

Use doubled embroidery thread when stitching on leather. When you sew through many thicknesses of leather, make a hole with an awl to allow the thread to go through easily. Be careful to keep all embroidery within 1-inch of the edges so that when you sew the two pillow pieces together you will not catch the embroidery stitching in the seam.

After finishing all embroidery stitching, place the right sides of the leather together, matching the edges. Machine stitch a ½-inch seam around three sides, and around both corners of the fourth side, leaving the remainder of this side open. Turn the pillow right side out and stuff it. Using waxed heavy cotton thread, close the opening by folding in the open edges and sewing them together with a hidden stitch (see fig. 198).

Directions for waxing your own thread can be found in the section on threads. Use the awl to make holes, if you have trouble sewing through the leather (plate 92).

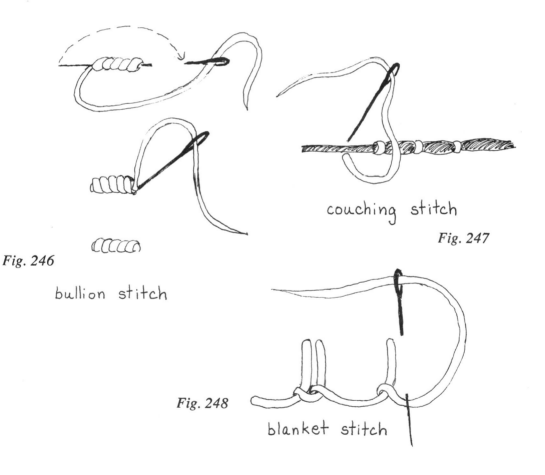

couching stitch

Fig. 247

Fig. 246

bullion stitch

Fig. 248

blanket stitch

Plate 92

TABLE COVERING

As neither suede nor felt are practical at dinner time, this table covering was made for purely decorative purposes.

MATERIALS

> Suede scraps
> Felt (used here: 2 yards long, 72-inches wide)
> Leather glue
> Scissors
> Chalk and string

CUTTING A CIRCLE

Fold the felt in half lengthwise and then in half again crosswise. Tie a long piece of string to a piece of chalk. Place the chalk at the point where the folded edges meet the open edges. Run the string tautly along this folded edge to the point where all folds meet. Holding the loose end of the string firmly at this point, swing the chalk across the felt to the other folds making a chalk line arc (fig. 249). Cut along this line with the felt still folded and you'll have a circle.

Place this circle fully open on a large flat surface.

Cut the shapes for the flower heads and place them around the middle area and outside the diameter of the table top. The cloth will not hang neatly if shapes are placed in the area where the felt meets the edge of the table. If you want to be sure this will not happen, cut a piece of paper the size of the table top and place it in the center of the cloth while you work (fig. 250).

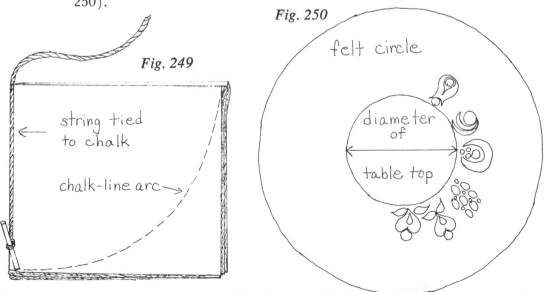

Fig. 250

Fig. 249

felt circle

string tied to chalk

chalk-line arc→

diameter of

table top

APPLIQUES

Flower forms are very basic when simplified. One form is to use circles in clusters, in rows or singly. Others include ovals pointed at one or both ends; half moons with or without rounded ends, free form shapes or squares with rounded edges. If you run out of ideas or need fresh ones, look for them in flower books or magazines.

First place the main flower shapes, then cut and place the stems, leaves, swirling vine shapes or any other forms you like.

Arrange and place all shapes before gluing them down (plates 93 and 94).

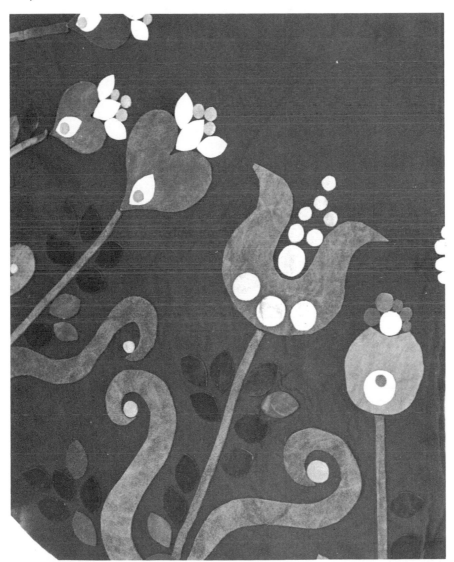

Plate 93

Plate 94

BED THROW

Pieces of leather scrap, not big enough to make any one-piece item and yet not small enough to throw away, would be suitable for making a bed throw. To make a large one, a great number of scraps are needed and could be collected over a long period of time. If you're not willing to wait until you have enough for a bed throw you might want to make something smaller. Anything can be made if you follow these steps in sewing the scraps together and then cut pattern pieces as you would from a length of material.

MATERIALS

Very large sheets of heavy paper
Leather scraps (large quantity)
Scissors
Tissue paper
Sewing machine
Leather glue
Masking tape
Heavy paper scraps (brown shopping bags)
Backing material (suggest cotton upholstery material)
Straight pins
Cotton filling or quilting batt (optional)

MAKING A PATTERN

Tape as many large sheets of paper together as necessary to make a pattern for a rectangular bed throw.

Draw your design on this paper pattern. Working a design in rows is the simplest method. Number each row (fig. 251). The pattern can be worked in one piece or the rows can be cut apart into separate patterns and worked one at a time. Leaving your pattern in one piece will help keep the rows straight.

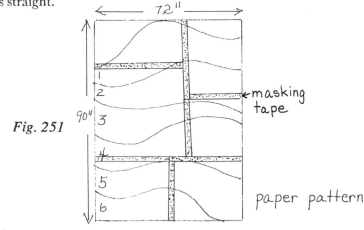

Fig. 251

WORKING THE ROWS

Cut all the pieces for the first row, overlapping them 1-inch at the side seams and 1-inch above and below the pen lines. Starting at one end, turn the pieces over and mark the row number and letter of each piece in sequence on the wrong side (plate 95). Keep these numbers running in one direction, making sure you do not turn the pieces upside-down as you flip them over to write the number. This way, you'll know which end is up.

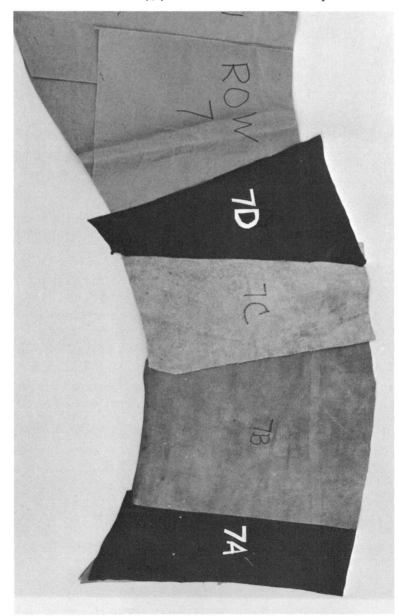

Plate 95

Matching the seam of piece 1-A with 1-B sew them together with a ½-inch seam using tissue paper between the machine and the leather. Now match the free edge of piece 1-B with 1-C and sew these two pieces together. Continue until this row is completely sewn together. Open and glue all seams flat (plate 96).

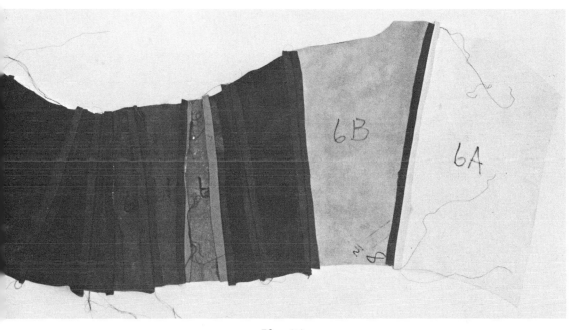

Plate 96

Repeat this process for the second row. To match the rows as accurately as possible, place the first row on the paper pattern while cutting the pieces for the next row. This is done because, as you sew the pieces of each row together, there is the possibility of distorting the curve (plate 97).

Once the second row is joined together, sew it to the first row along the curve line by turning the edges of the second row under and topstitching it to the first row (fig. 252). Use heavy brown paper strips between the leather and the machine in this instance, because they tear away cleaner. Try to follow the curves as accurately as possible. This is a very difficult seam to make. To avoid ripping out and resewing, it is important to match each row (as you cut them) to the previously sewn rows.

Plate 97

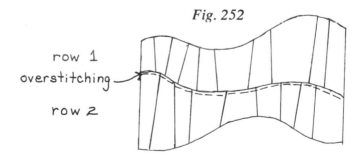

Fig. 252

row 1
overstitching
row 2

When all the rows are sewn together, place the partly finished throw on the paper pattern and cut any pieces necessary to fill in the areas at the top, bottom or sides to complete the rectangle (fig. 253).

When finished, the leather layer, by itself, is very heavy. Since any quilting or backing you add will make it heavier, you might prefer simply to hem all edges, leaving one side unfinished. If you are planning a layer of quilting, do not topstitch after you have finished the third row. Instead, follow this topstitching procedure after you have added the quilting.

Fig. 253

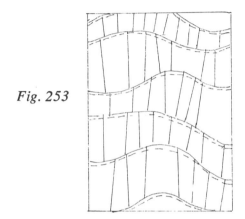

BACKING THE BED THROW

The bed throw can be backed with any strong material. If you want to eliminate the rough feel of the seam lines, place quilting or cotton batting on the wrong side. This must be sewn down in various spots or it will rip away later and create lumps. Before sewing, glue the quilting in place in 8-inch squares both horizontally and vertically. Using paper to protect both leather and quilting, stitch by following each curve across the width of the bed throw. Then stitch along wedge edges to reinforce the quilting vertically. Roll your quilt up at either end and sew carefully and slowly to prevent ripping the cotton quilting. Place the backing material on top of the quilting. Lay it out on a large flat area. Fold the edges under to meet evenly and pin them together before sewing (fig. 254). Be sure the leather is stretched out fully while doing this. Again stitch together (using a long stitch) with the leather facing you and with brown paper between the leather and the machine.

To give the piece a really finished look whipstitch the edges together by hand (fig. 255 and plate 98).

If you would like to simplify the whole procedure, you can use an old blanket which will not have to be overstitched to keep it in place.

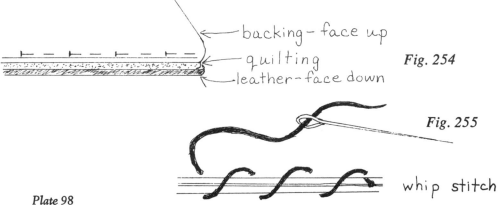

backing – face up
quilting   *Fig. 254*
leather – face down

Fig. 255

whip stitch

Plate 98

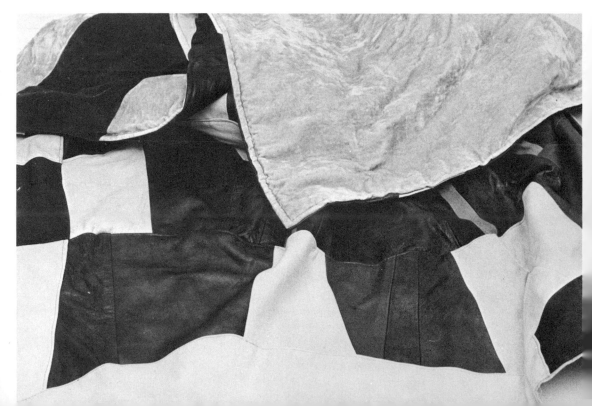

5. Fur Fashions

WORKING WITH FURS

FURRIERS' TOOLS

Furriers' knife: Designed for cutting so that only the point pierces skin. It's easy to hold and will not damage fur, as a mat knife, for instance, might.

Cold tape: Special tape with one sticky side; used to strengthen edges.

Furriers' thread: Silk for strength.

Glovers' needles: Have extra sharp point; prevents catching and ripping skin because it makes a clean hole.

WORKING METHODS

1. Always cut fur on the wrong side, never the fur side.

2. Pierce the *skin only* with the tip of the blade. Never cut deeply as this will chop off the hairs.

3. For best results use a furriers' knife.

4. Always use cold tape on all edges.

5. Use triple pointed (actually 3 flat sides) glovers' needles. The widened, flat sides open the hole allowing the thread to go through with less stress than an ordinary needle would cause.

6. Use silk thread (specifically, furriers' thread). It's stronger and usually finer.

7. Flaws and holes must be repaired before beginning on the item.

   A. SMALL HOLES (SEE FUR MUFF FOR DIAGRAMS): Slit through the hole from ½-inch above it, to 2-inches below it. Place cold tape on both edges. Sew these edges together with overcast stitches ⅛-inch apart.

   B. LARGE HOLES OR SCARS (PULLING A TRIANGLE): Cut a square out around the hole or scar. Below this cut out a long triangle. Move this triangle up to the top of the cut out portion. Place cold tape on all edges including the triangle edges. Sew around all edges with an overcast stitch.

8. To create an impression of one large piece of fur sew the smaller pieces together with the fur running in one direction.

9. When lining up pelts, especially when you are going to square them off or cut a pattern from them, center the pelts for strength. The side edges are generally weaker and may rip.

10. After repairs are made and all pieces in a section are sewn together, the section must be blocked to flatten lumps or bumps caused by repairing and sewing.

    a. Staple the section along all edges, fur side down, to a flat workboard.

    b. If the pelts are new dampen the back with water; never soak.

    c. If you're working with old fur dampen the back with alcohol; again, never soak.

    d. When thoroughly dry remove the staples.

FAKE FURS

The fake furs on the market today not only come in a surprising variety of textures, but happily, they also feel like real fur. They are made from various synthetics and have a knitted or woven backing. Besides offering a large choice of animal patterns they also offer a variety of piles ranging from flat to very deep or long-haired.

To work with fake furs, a combination of fur techniques and cloth sewing techniques can be used.

As you do when working with real fur, the pattern should be laid on the fabric in one direction. Although most furs look their best when cut with the pile running down, you can achieve interesting effects like a shaggier look (with long hair) or a more exciting pattern (when it's leopard or a similar design), by running the pile upward. Determine how your fabric looks best before you begin to cut. When purchasing the fabric, check to see if it will wear well by folding it and examining this fold. If the hairs seem far apart it will probably wear out quickly. Extra fabric is often needed because markings or textures must be matched. Purchase enough fabric to follow the cutting layout labeled "with nap." When cutting long-haired fabric use a single-edge razor blade on the wrong side of the fabric. Do not push the blade in deep. To prevent chopping off the fur, slit only the backing and cut through one thickness at a time. Avoid folding deep-piled furs when cutting. Short-piled furs can be cut with a scissors, but there will be some fuzz, so choose to work in an area that will sweep up easily.

To prevent puckering and to assure that the fabric will go through the machine evenly, hand baste all seams before stitching. Use a long stitch and a heavy-duty thread with a looser tension than usual and less pressure on the presser foot.

Stitch in the direction of the nap whenever possible. Seam tape should be used on all areas where there will be stress. Pull out any hairs caught in the seam line, using a pin.

Some fake furs tend to shred easily when cut, so don't clip curved seams too close to the stitching line. Darts should be sewn with all the material left in and slashed down the middle after being sewn. For the same reason, avoid cutting out notches, and instead mark them on the wrong side of the fabric in tailors' chalk. To further prevent fraying, finish all seams and edges with 1¼-inch bias strips (meaning strips cut on the bias, from another material, or bias tape which comes in 1-inch widths. Place one strip on a seam edge, right sides together. Machine stitch them together ¼-inch from the edge (fig. 256). Turn this sewn edge to the wrong side of the fabric and machine-stitch it flat (see fig. 257). Flatten the entire seam and hand hem it flat.

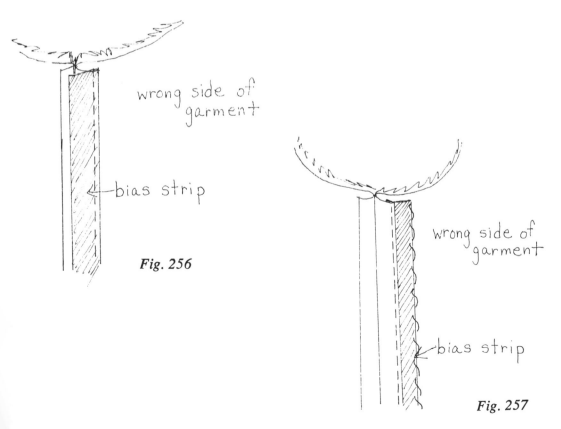

wrong side of garment

←bias strip

Fig. 256

wrong side of garment

←bias strip

Fig. 257

Long-haired fabric has a special problem; too much bulk. You will save yourself a lot of hassling by avoiding buttonholes and substituting hooks and eyes or decorative closings. Eliminate unnecessary seam lines wherever possible. For instance the front edge facing can be attached to the front piece and cut as one, instead of two separate pieces, or use another thinner fabric for facings. Shearing the pile off all seam allowances will also remove excess bulk.

Sew in the lining, following pattern directions. If you plan to use the fur fabric as a lining be sure you have enlarged your pattern before cutting. How much larger the garment will have to be, will depend on the bulkiness of the fabric.

Pressing seams should be done on a needle board. This is a piece of canvas stretched over a board covered with thin wires which stand up from the canvas. Ironing on this will prevent the fabric from flattening and matting. Practice this technique on a scrap of fabric. Press the pile side onto the wires and cover the wrong side with a steam iron pressing cloth. Do not touch the fabric with the iron but press it by getting the iron as close as possible to it without *touching* and let the steam do the work.

Some synthetic furs are washable, others must be dry-cleaned. Follow the manufacturer's directions in care and cleaning of your fabric.

Care, Cleaning and Storage of Furs

Usually when you've completed a fur piece, it is finished by ironing and glazing. Because it is very easy to burn the hair, I would suggest that you do not iron it yourself, but send it out to be done. Also, send it out whenever it needs a good cleaning.

Glazing is a process that makes the fur shine, which also helps fluff it up. Commercially this is usually done by machines, but you can glaze fur by hand, although you will probably never get the high shine that the professionals do. To glaze, begin by brushing the fur in the direction it grows with a medium fine bristle brush that has been dipped in water. Never put water directly on the fur. You want to wet the fur, only, without getting the skin wet. Now take a glazing stick (a long stick of wax) and brush the fur up with it, against the direction that the fur grows. Do this in short quick strokes hitting a little of the fur at a time. This will make the fur stand out a bit. Let the fur dry in this position.

There are procedures you can follow at home to prolong the life of your furs and to keep them looking good. All fur garments should be hung on wooden shoulder hangers. When fur gets wet, simply shake it out and hang it away by itself where it won't get crushed or crowded by other garments or flattened by leaning up against something, like a wall. Never put fur near heat, especially when drying, and if possible, store fur pelts in a cool place until you're ready to use them.

FUR MUFF

I'd like to include the basics you need to work with fur, since there are some differences between it and leather. Fur is the pelt with the hair still on and not yet tanned. The tanning process removes the hair. Some skins are not suitable for tanning because they are too thin.

Rabbit, Persian lamb, kidskin with the hair left on and sheepskin are the furs which are usually used to work large projects because they don't require complicated cuts. Take into account the shape and size of the animal, and the possible waste when cutting around a scruffy neck or tail area, at the time you choose the furs. Also, check the pieces carefully for bald spots, holes and flaws. Select the most perfect pieces.

MATERIALS

2 large rabbit pelts (4, if small)
Furriers' knife and blades (get split blades from a furriers' supplier)
Cold tape (silk tape with one sticky side)
1 yard grosgrain ribbon to match fur
Muff bed
Furriers' thread (machine silk, size B)
Fur needle (glovers' needle, size 6, triple pointed)
Denatured alcohol (needed only if working with old fur)
Sponge
Heavy paper for pattern
Tailors' chalk

CUTTING FUR

Fur is always cut on the hide side, not on the fur side. Pierce the skin only with the tip of your blade. If you make a deep cut, you'll also cut the hairs (fig. 258). Use very sharp blades and hold the blade at an angle.

underside
of fur

←furrier's knife

Fig. 258

REPAIRING HOLES

If the piece does have holes, they must be repaired. To repair a small hole, slit through it from about ½-inch above it to about 2-inches below it. Because the hole is so small, the excess will be taken up as you sew (fig. 259). Now place cold tape on both edges for strength and sew them together with an overcast stitch. The stitches should be very close together—no more than ⅛-inch apart (fig. 260). This method prevents large bumps from being formed.

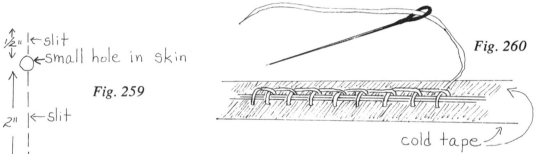

½"|←slit

←small hole in skin

Fig. 259

2"|←slit

Fig. 260

cold tape

When repairing larger holes cut out a square around the hole. Below this cut out a long triangle (fig. 261). Move this triangle up to the top of the cut out portion (fig. 262). Place cold tape on all edges close to the edge, and sew it in with an overcast stitch. This process is called pulling a triangle. Use only furrier's thread and needle. If you use other types there is a chance you'll tear the fur and the thread may break.

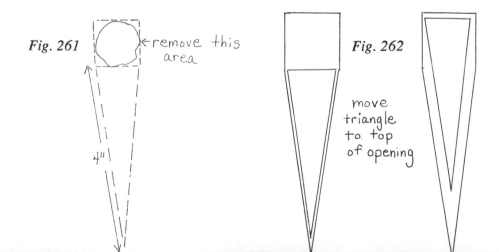

Fig. 261

←remove this area

4"

Fig. 262

move triangle to top of opening

Preparing The Pieces To Be Sewn Together

To cut your main pieces you must clear away the head and tail area by cutting them off. The area around the tail grows in many directions and is rough. Cut off those areas that will not lie flat, squaring off your piece as you do so.

A good 1-inch or more must be cut off the sides (flanks) of the skin because this is the weakest area and will eventually rip if used (fig. 263). When you have finished cutting, each piece will be a rectangle.

Line the skins up vertically, placing them one below the other neck to tail (fig. 264). This keeps the fur running in one direction and helps conceal seams.

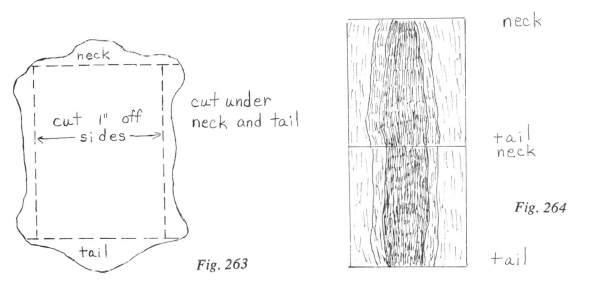

cut under
neck and tail

Fig. 263

Fig. 264

When you buy pelts, try to match the colors. Arrange the pelts by matching the center backs of the skins. On a rabbit, the center back is usually a darker colored stripe. If you place the pieces off-center, in an attempt to save fur, the color will not match and flow into the next piece. This flow makes it appear to be one large piece. Also, the strongest part of the pelt is the center because the skin gets progressively thinner towards the sides.

Once lined up, place cold tape on the two edges to be sewn together and again sew with an overcast stitch (fig. 265).

STRETCHING THE PELTS

Staple this piece to a flat work board with the fur down. If your pelts are new, dampen the back with water. Do not soak. If you're working with an old coat use denatured alcohol. Using water on old skins will deteriorate them. Alcohol dries quickly and thus lessens the danger of damage. Dampening the skin flattens and removes bumps by causing it to shrink slightly. Let it dry fully.

The size of the rectangle made by the pelts and the muff bed you choose will determine the finished size of the muff. They come in 3 sizes for rounded muffs like this one; 10 x 20-inches, 11 x 22-inches and 12 x 24-inches. There is also a flat muff bed. Buy this item *before* cutting your muff pattern from fur. If you find that the two skins sewn together will not be enough to go across the width of the muff bed, sew two more skins together in the same way and then sew the two pieces together vertically (fig. 266). Choose the muff bed that is closest in size but smaller than your sewn skins. A muff bed is a lining with a zipper section that serves as a purse.

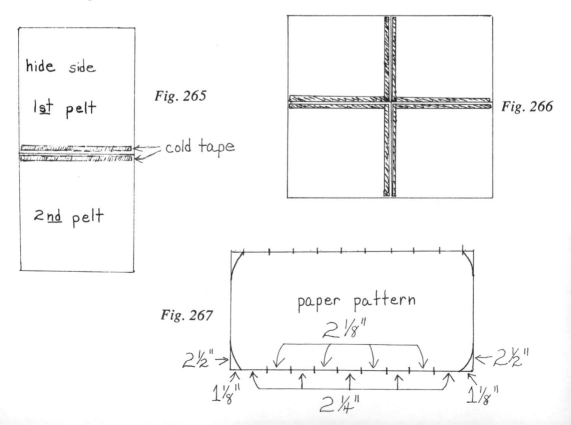

hide side

1st pelt

Fig. 265

cold tape

2nd pelt

Fig. 266

Fig. 267

paper pattern

2 ⅛"

2½"→

←2½"

1⅛"

2¼"

1⅛"

CUTTING A MUFF PATTERN

To make a pattern for an 11 x 22-inch rounded muff, cut a paper rectangle that size. Draw a curve on each corner beginning $2\frac{1}{2}$-inches in on the short side of the rectangle, to $1\frac{1}{8}$-inch in on each long side. On each long side, mark off $2\frac{1}{4}$-inches, $2\frac{1}{8}$-inches, $2\frac{1}{4}$-inches, $2\frac{1}{8}$-inches, etc. until you reach the end of the side (fig. 267). Now, $2\frac{1}{2}$-inches in from the edge, place marks midway between each $2\frac{1}{8}$-inch section. Mark and cut curves to these inner marks (fig. 268).

Place this pattern on the dried stretched skins and mark around it with tailors' chalk. Remove the staples and cut along the chalk lines with your blade. Put cold tape on all remaining edges. Overcast adjacent curved edges, joining them together (figs. 269 and 270). (Note: cold tape is available at furrier supply shops.)

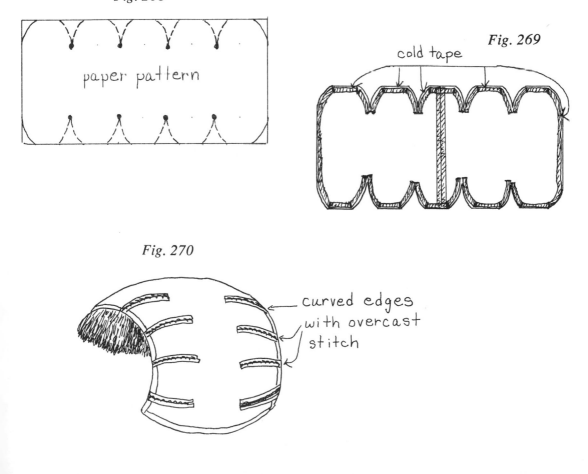

Fig. 268

paper pattern

Fig. 269

cold tape

Fig. 270

curved edges with overcast stitch

Sew grosgrain ribbon on the openings for your hands, with the ribbon placed against the fur side (fig. 271). Sew the remaining horizontal seam together. If you want to try sewing the seams on a sewing machine practice with a scrap piece first. Because the stitching must be very close to the edges, the machine may tear the fur or catch it unevenly. Sewing the fur by hand is, therefore, much safer. Furriers use an expensive sewing machine which does not catch or tear the pelts.

To finish the muff, turn the ribbon to the inside, fit the muff bed inside and hand-stitch it to the grosgrain ribbon exactly where the ribbon meets the fur (plate 99).

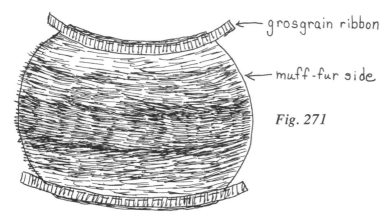

grosgrain ribbon

muff-fur side

Fig. 271

Plate 99

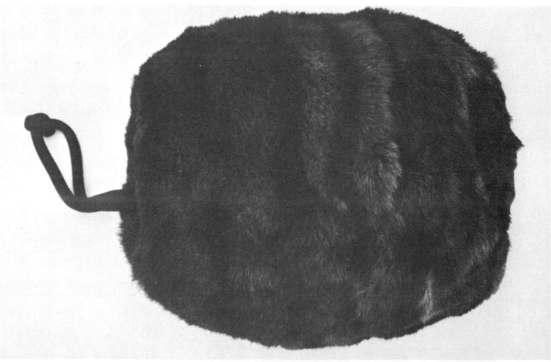

SHEEPSKIN-LINED VEST

This vest was adapted from the pattern used for the long fringed vest by cutting it shorter, curving it in on the front edges and adding closing tabs and pockets (fig. 272).

One sheepskin may be enough but to be certain, take your pattern with you when purchasing them.

MATERIALS

    Reversible suede skin
    2 sheepskins (used here: combed and bleached)
    Pattern
    Leather glue
    Scissors
    Sewing machine
    Brown paper strips

When cutting the pattern, allow for the bulky lining by cutting all the pieces larger. If you wish to work with a different pattern, choose a simple one. Try to avoid darts and too many seam lines.

Attach your pattern to the inside of the sheepskin with masking tape. If the pattern has a center back fold do not fold the skin to cut it—instead flip the pattern at the center back, so that you can cut through a single thickness of sheepskin (fig. 273). Cut all sheepskin pieces the way described for fur, on the inside with a sharp razor blade. Add at least 1-inch on all side and shoulder seams, front and bottom edges. Cut neck and armhole edges along the stitching lines. Cut linings for the pockets.

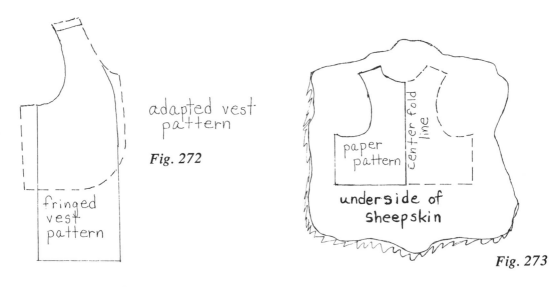

adapted vest pattern

Fig. 272

fringed vest pattern

paper pattern   center fold line

underside of sheepskin

Fig. 273

Cut all suede pieces the same size as you cut the sheepskin pieces. Cut 4 tabs and 2 pockets (fig. 274). Pin all pieces together, overlapping seams; check to be sure it fits. If it's too big, trim accordingly.

Glue the sheepskin pocket to the suede pocket, wrong sides together. Match the edges carefully. Trim if necessary. Place the pockets, on the front suede pieces, with the fur side down and spaced far enough away from the side seams. Pull the wool out beyond the pocket edges. Sew pockets in place with the longest machine stitch you have, or use waxed thread and sew them on by hand. Use brown paper strips to protect both surfaces when machine sewing.

Glue two flaps together suede sides out. Use a razor blade to cut buttonholes through them. Sew these in place on the right vest front. Sew buttons on the left vest front being sure they're in the proper position to match the buttonholes on the flaps.,

Machine or hand-stitch suede front pieces to suede back piece at the shoulders only, by overlapping the front seam edges over the back seam edges (fig. 275). The stitching will show. Shear the wool from the seam allowances on the shoulder seams of the sheepskin. Sew these seams together, matching the sheared edges carefully (fig. 276).

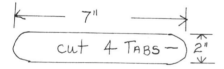

Fig. 274

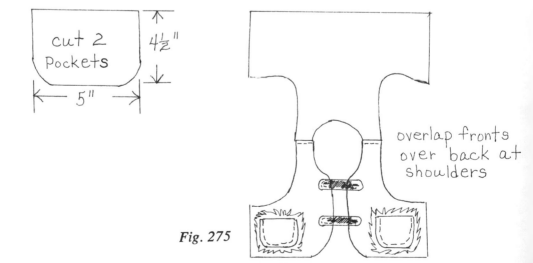

Fig. 275

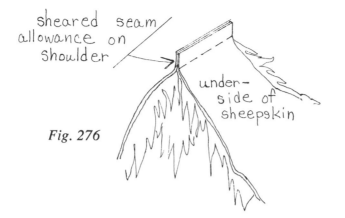

sheared seam allowance on shoulder

under-side of sheepskin

Fig. 276

Glue the sheepskin lining to the suede shell along the neck, armhole, side seam, front and bottom edges.

Overlap the front side seams onto the back side seams and stitch them together with the sheepskin facing you. Separate the wool away from the stitching line as you work, being careful not to catch the wool on this side (fig. 277). Be sure you have arranged the wool on the other side of the vest so that it sticks out at the side seams and is caught when stitching.

Sheepskin has a very nicely finished inside. A vest could be made using the smooth side as the outside of the vest, and decorating it with paint, ink or magic marker design (plate 100).

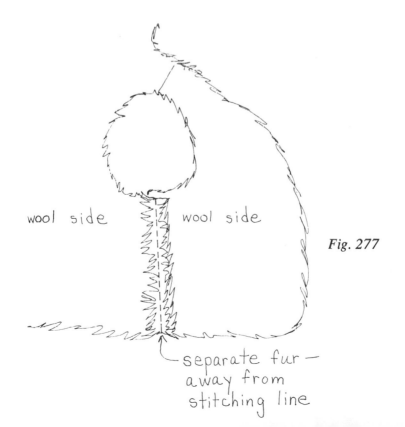

wool side   wool side

Fig. 277

─ separate fur ─ away from stitching line

Plate 100

FOXTAIL FRINGED SHAWL

This shawl is designed in a complete circle that will fold over to create a double-tiered effect in the back. Three cow-splits are needed to make a circle. The size of the circle will vary according to the size of the skins. Its maximum diameter will be between 52-inches and 56-inches depending on the length of your arms. It can be smaller if you wish.

MATERIALS

    3 large suede split cowhides
    22 fox tails (or other tails)
    Revolving punch
    Scissors
    Cold tape
    Furriers' knife
    Furriers' needle and thread
    Steel straightedge
    Chalk and string
    Awl

Choose suede pieces that are unmarred on both sides and have the same coloring on both sides. Lay them uncut on a large, flat surface to determine the best way to put them together to make the circle. Lay them all lengthwise and overlapping.

Measure the width of your shoulders across the back. Cut the middle piece of suede into a long strip as wide as this measurement. You will now have straight edges which will be cross-laced to the two side pieces later. Place this piece in the middle, overlapping the other two pieces (fig. 278). Straighten the other rough edges by using the straight edges of the middle piece as guides. Do not cut off more than is absolutely necessary.

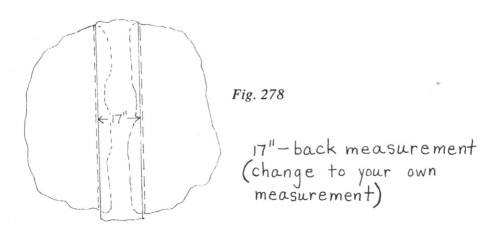

Fig. 278

17" – back measurement
(change to your own
measurement)

Single rows of holes must be punched along all straightened edges with the exception of a span of 14-inches which will be left open for your arms. This opening must be much closer to one side than the other. Using an imaginary line that makes a 90° angle to the straightened edges to indicate the middle of the shawl leave 3-inches open above this center line and 11-inches open below this center line (fig. 279). Do not punch holes in these areas.

After determining where the arm slits will be located and checking to be sure they're parallel, punch your lacing holes. Match the single rows of holes on each adjacent straight edge so that the pieces will lace evenly. Start the cross-lacing from the arm slits and work towards the outer edges (fig. 280). Do not lace all the way to the edges, but just enough to hold the 3 pieces together.

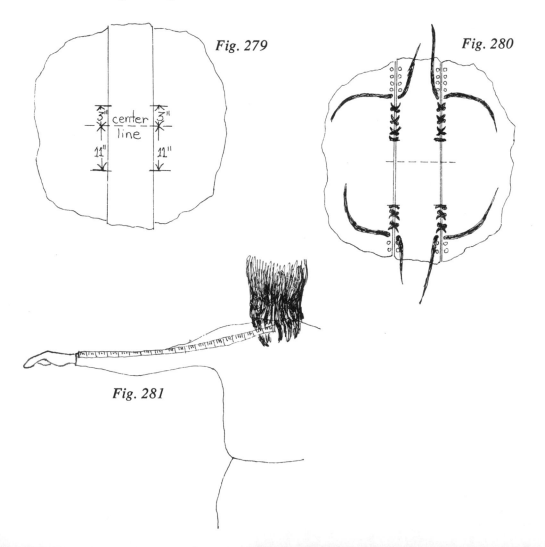

Fig. 279

center line

3" 3"

11" 11"

Fig. 280

Fig. 281

Hold your arm straight out and have someone measure from the center of your neck to your wrist (fig. 281). Mark this measurement onto the suede from the center of the unmarked line (or mark it with a string) used to make the arm slits. Using chalk tied to a long string, place the chalk on the arm measurement mark and run the string tautly to this center mark. Hold it on the mark while you swing the chalk around to make a circle keeping the string taut (fig. 282). Cut along this chalk line. Finish cross-lacing the straight edges.

Prepare the foxtails by opening them at the top with your fingers. Cut them straight and apply a piece of cold tape to each edge (fig. 283). Place them around the edge of the circle with the fur against the right side of the suede and the tip of the tail pointing toward the center of the shawl (fig. 284). Sew each in place with furrier's needle and thread (fig. 285). If the

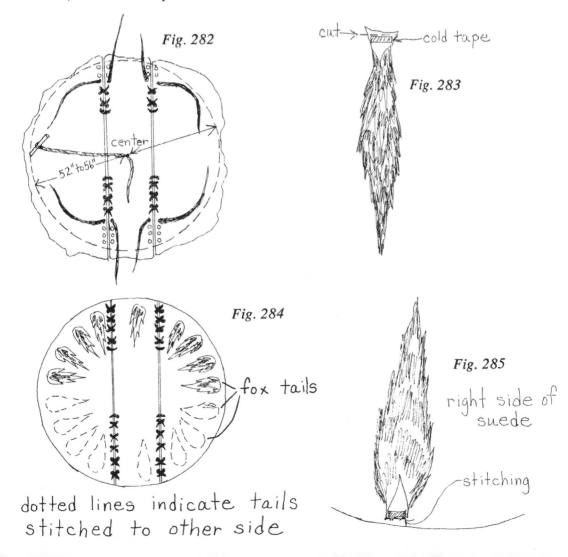

Fig. 282

center

52" to 56"

cut → cold tape

Fig. 283

Fig. 284

fox tails

Fig. 285

right side of suede

stitching

dotted lines indicate tails stitched to other side

needle won't go through the suede easily, make holes with an awl first. Remember when placing them that the right side changes when the upper tier is folded onto your back. Sew tails accordingly.

Swinging tails may be made by sewing them to long thongs threaded through double sets of holes. Prepare the edge as before with cold tape, but fold this edge of the tail around itself. Round off the thong ends and place them around the tail facing each other. Sew through all thicknesses securely (fig. 286 and plate 101).

EASY FUR PROJECTS

Try a fur pillow by following directions for the pillow in this book, but apply the special techniques for working with fur that are listed.

Try a fur throw rug by piecing together 2 or more fur pelts. Follow directions for the fur muff, but leave the outer edges as they naturally are for a casual look (fig. 287).

Try fur belts, fur purse, fur spats, combining fur and leather. In fact you could make almost any item in this book in fur if you use the special techniques for working with fur.

Plate 101

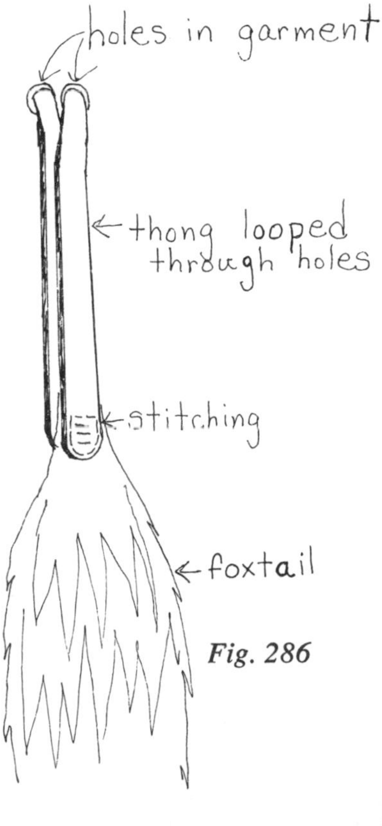

Fig. 286

RECYCLED FUR RUG

You can easily find an out-of-style fur coat at a thrift shop or rummage sale, with plenty of good, usable fur in it. Persian lamb, muskrat, sheared beaver . . . any of these would make an interesting rug. If you can't bear to walk on it, after you have completed it, hang it on the wall.

The pelts of an old fur coat are already cut and pieced together, therefore, it would be better to cut the coat into squares or rectangles no larger than 15 inches in any one direction. By piecing together many small squares rather than cutting one or two big ones, you can eliminate worn spots and badly ripped areas and avoid lumpy tailored areas (like darts or curves) so that your rug lies flat. A smaller square is also easier to shrink evenly. Before cutting, plan the way you'll cut the squares to be sure that you'll have enough to make the shape rug you want.

Using the fur techniques previously described in both the section on general fur directions and those given for making a fur muff, cut the fur on the hide side; stretch and shrink each piece; place cold tape around all the edges of each piece; use furrier's thread to sew the pieces together.

If you'd like to back any of the fur projects, sew grosgrain ribbon around the outer edges of the piece with the ribbon against the fur side. (see fig. 271) Choose a material which will not stretch and which is soil resistant. If you'd like it to be reversible, choose an attractive color or print for lining. Once sewn around the edges, turn the ribbon to the inside of the piece. Fit your lining material to cover the wrong side and hand stitch it in place to the ribbon (see lining the fur muff).

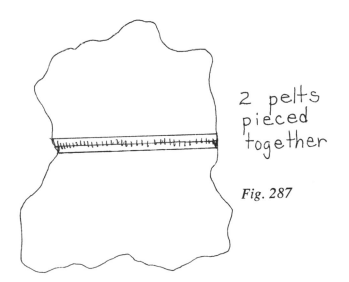

2 pelts pieced together

Fig. 287

6. Creativity in Leather

WEAVING WITH LEATHER

Your loom can be any size your ambition allows. The larger it is, the more time and materials you'll need. Mine is a good beginner's size, 8½ x 11-inches. It took 6 hours to complete the weaving.

MATERIALS

> ⅛-inch thick cardboard for loom
> Thin cardboard for shuttle
> Mat knife or single-edged razor blade
> Scissors
> String for warp threads
> Suede and leather scraps
> Wools and twine of varied thicknesses
> Aluminum foil
> Comb for beater
> Tacks
> 2 strips heavy cardboard, each one-inch-wide
> ¾-inch dowel or heavy twig (1½-inches longer than top of loom)
> Brown wax or liquid shoe polish
> Paper towel

MAKING THE LOOM

To set up your loom, draw a line ½-inch from the edge, and parallel to the top and bottom of your heavy cardboard. Mark off ¼-inch spaces along both lines. Cut points between the dots with your mat knife, single-edge razor blade or heavy scissors.

SETTING UP THE LOOM

Pass string through the first notch at the top leaving a piece hanging over the back. Bring the string down and loop it around the first point at the bottom of the board. Bring it up to the top of the board again and loop it around the next point. Continue until you've looped the string around all the points (fig. 288).

Keep the string taut as you wind it on. Bring the last string around the back and tie it tightly to the beginning string (fig. 289). These vertical strings are called warp threads.

Place the 1-inch strips of heavy cardboard between the loom and the warp strings, pushing these strips as close to the ends of the board as possible (fig. 290). This raises the warp threads making it easier to pass the weft threads through. The weft threads are all horizontal threads or strips.

THE SHUTTLE

Make a shuttle by cutting keyhole shapes into both ends of a thinner piece of cardboard (fig. 291). If the cardboard is very light, double it to give it strength. Wrap as much yarn around it as you'll need for the first color.

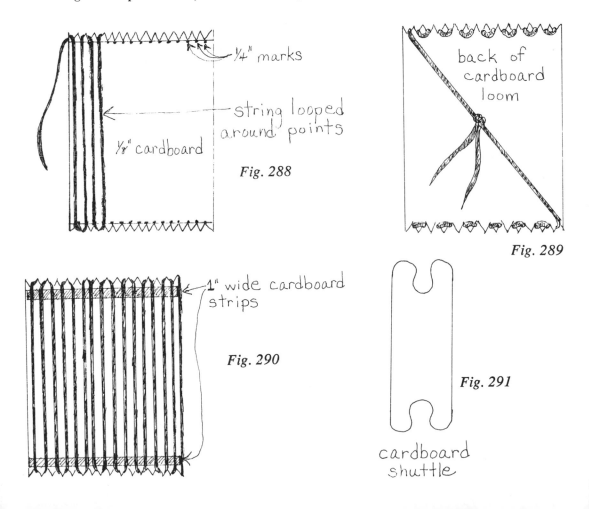

¼" marks

string looped around points

⅛" cardboard

Fig. 288

back of cardboard loom

Fig. 289

1" wide cardboard strips

Fig. 290

Fig. 291

cardboard shuttle

WEAVING

Beginning about ½-inch from the bottom edge and 5 or 6 warp strings in from the side edge, pass the shuttle under one string and over the next (fig. 292). When you reach the end warp string, loop the weft thread around it and continue passing over one and under the next, across the entire row. Repeat weaving back and forth through the warp threads. After each row use the comb to beat the threads close to the row before it. Continue with this thread until you have a stripe as wide as you want. To end using this color, pass the thread back through 5 or 6 warp strings and cut it off.

There are many different ways to vary this pattern to make your piece more interesting. The basic method is to vary the thickness of the yarns, twines or strips of leather. But whatever you use, the procedure is much the same. Passing the weft threads over 1 warp string and under 3 or using any variation in the number of strings passed, is another way to vary the patterns.

There are two ways to give a woven piece strength. Either use a close weave such as under one, over one, etc. Or, use alternate rows of yarn and leather strips.

WEAVING WITH LEATHER

It is not necessary to use the shuttle when weaving with suede or leather. Cut strips as wide or as thin as you like. Try cutting holes or shapes out of a very wide strip before weaving it in. Always cut them an inch or two longer than is necessary for one pass across the row. Instead of starting them as you would yarn, simply push the leather strip through with your fingers and cut the excess off the sides.

WEAVING WITH ALUMINUM FOIL

When using aluminum foil cut as many 1-inch-wide strips as you need. Fold or twist them lengthwise into any thickness you like.

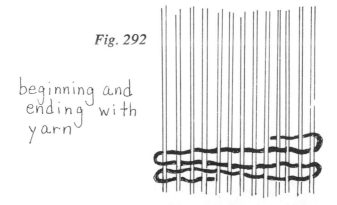

Fig. 292

beginning and
ending with
yarn

WEAVING CIRCLES

If you're going to use circles in your design, weave these in before you complete too much of the cross-weaving. Areas around these circles are filled in later as you get to them. To make a circle with aluminum foil, twist one end of the aluminum foil strip around one warp string at least 6 strings in from the edge of the loom. Weave in a circular direction instead of straight across. Don't be afraid to pull the warp strings close together even though it will also pull them out of line. This will not be noticeable when you weave around the circle later. If you're using yarn, tie it on, keeping the knot on the wrong side of the woven piece (fig. 293).

FRINGE AND TASSELS

Fringe is made by wrapping yarn around a piece of cardboard, a paperback book or a small box. The size of that item will determine the length of the fringe. Wrap quite a bit. (For instance, I wrapped 50 times around to get enough fringe to loop over 10 warp threads.) Slip it off and cut through both ends. Take about 10 strands and fold them in half, forming a loop. Place the loop on top of one warp string. Pass the ends under and around that string and pass them up through the loop (fig. 294). Pull as tightly as possible and push it as close to the last row as possible. Trim each fringe to the desired length as soon as it has been tied on. Remember that the longer the fringe the more the previously woven pattern will be covered up. When finished with the entire row, comb the fringe as you would hair. One variation of this process is to clip one short and one long; another is tassels, which are added after the piece is finished and off the loom.

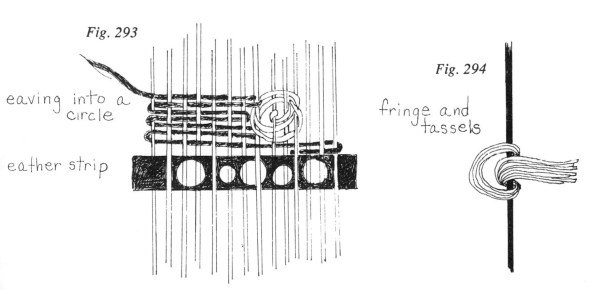

Fig. 293

eaving into a circle

eather strip

Fig. 294

fringe and tassels

Herringbone Weave

To start the herringbone stitch begin the row as you normally would, 5 or 6 warp threads from the edge. When you reach the last string, loop the weft thread around it by passing the thread under it first, then one full turn around it, and when you come around to the top again, carry it immediately to the second warp string. Wrap it around this string once and on to the next warp string. This forms a series of loose knots. Push each knot down as you wind, so that the thread between each warp string slants down. When you have reached the opposite end, repeat the stitch in the other direction. To form this pattern you need at least 2 rows (fig. 295).

Filling In Around Circles

As you work up the board you'll eventually reach the bottom of the circle (or one of the circles). To fill in the areas around it, weave as close to the circle as possible and then weave back. Do this on both sides of the circle until all the areas around it are filled in and you're able to weave full rows across again.

As you weave, the tendency is to pull each row tighter until the piece looks bowed in the middle. Sometimes this can be attractive. But, if you want a perfectly straight edge, push tacks into the loom board at intervals to hold each end string in place (fig. 296).

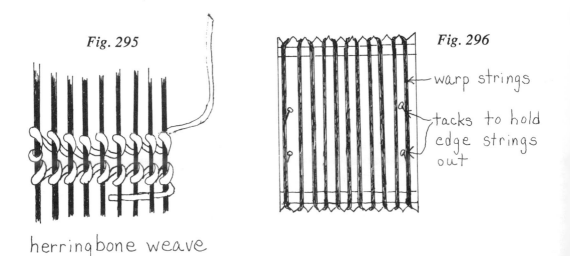

Fig. 295

Fig. 296

warp strings

tacks to hold edge strings out

herringbone weave

Apply shoe polish to the wood dowel with a paper towel and rub it in well.

When you get to within ½-inch of the top, slip the loops off one at a time and transfer them to the dowel or twig.

Take the bottom loops off and add tassels.

Cut the back string and tie each end onto the closed loop.

To hang it up, tie each end of a piece of string to each end of the dowel (plate 102).

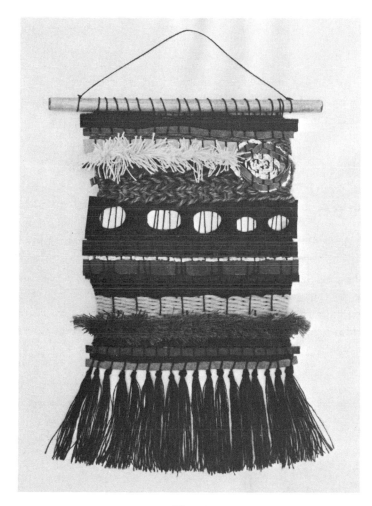

Plate 102

LEATHER AND SHELL COLLAGE

MATERIALS

> Backing board (used here: ceiling tile cut to 24 x 30-inches
> Reversible cowhide (3-inches larger than the board all around)
> Leather and suede scraps
> White glue (used here: Elmer's glue)
> Assorted shells (used here: about 400)
> Scissors
> Toothpicks
> Cotton swabs

COVERING THE BACKING BOARD

Cover the backing board by spreading white glue over the entire front surface a little at a time. Spread the glue in 2- or 3-inch-wide sections. Center the leather on the board. Flip down about 4-inches of one top (or bottom) edge. Apply glue to exposed board. After applying one section of glue, press down firmly on this area, flattening the leather and spreading any glue that may be too thick (fig. 297).

When you've finished with the entire front of the board apply glue to one outside edge at a time. Press as you did before and cut a slit from the outside corner of the leather to the front corner of the board, as you do each side (fig. 298).

There will be an excess at the corners when the leather is folded onto the back of the board. To eliminate bulk when gluing, cut this excess off at a 45° angle, so that both edges meet and from a miter when pasted down.

If you haven't decided on a subject, you may get an idea by separating the shells into types, sizes and colors.

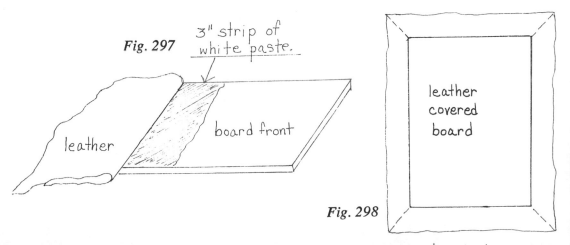

Fig. 297 3" strip of white paste.

leather

board front

Fig. 298 leather covered board

cut all 4 corners

Once you have decided upon the subject, cut the main leather pieces that are going to comprise your picture (in my collage; the face, eyes, mouth and hair). Place, but do not glue them where they belong in your design.

ARRANGING SHELLS

Arrange the shells. To obtain the mosaic effect in the collar, I used many of the same kind and size shell. Special one-of-a-kind shells make the cluster for the crown and rows of butterfly shells form stripes in the dress.

I then cut pieces of suede for the dress, to fill in the empty areas and complete the picture.

Some pieces may need to be picked up and trimmed to fit, cut to correct proportions. Do this now, before starting to glue the pieces down.

PASTING SHELLS

Apply glue to the area of the shell which will touch the board. If the area is small, like the rim around a shell edge it might be easier to apply the paste with a toothpick or cotton swab (plate 103).

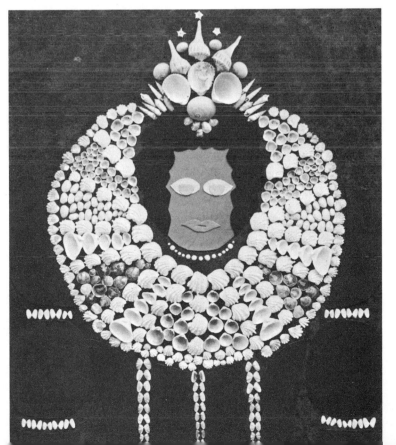

Plate 103

While a ceiling tile is a very convenient and lightweight backing to use, it does have drawbacks. Picture screw eyes of the kind normally used to hang a work of this size, will not hold in the tile. You can solve this problem in one of two ways. A professional picture frame can be added or you can press two very thin, long nails almost all the way into the side edges and wrap picture wire around them so that the collage can be hung (fig. 299).

Fig. 299

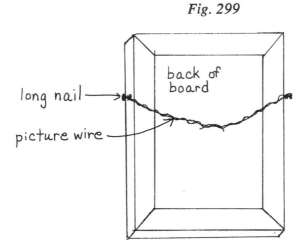

PADDED APPLIQUE NUDE

Padded appliqué is a very interesting way to obtain a three-dimensional effect. To do this, selected pieces of the design are partially sewn down, stuffed with a soft material and then sewn around the open edges.

MATERIALS

Background piece (used here: 1 full split-suede navy blue cowhide)
Large and small leather scraps (used here: tans and browns)
Scrap fur
Stuffing: old stockings, soft fabric scraps, wool scraps or cotton batting
Leather glue
Sewing machine
Thread (heavy duty, mercerized)
Large brown paper scraps
Awl for hand sewing
Sharp needles for hand sewing
Beads

Lay your large backing piece on a flat surface. Cut your design from paper if you're not positive about it or if you want to experiment before cutting from leather. As you cut these pieces decide which ones you want to leave flat and which will be padded.

PADDED APPLIQUE

Cut your suede and leather pieces accordingly and lay them in place on the backing piece. Cut all pieces to be padded slightly larger than the size you want them to be. This will allow the leather to raise when you stuff it. Glue down thoroughly, those pieces which are to be flat. Be sure such pieces are not overlapping any of the pieces to be padded. If desired, you may also sew them in place for a more decorative effect.

Now glue the pieces to be padded, only halfway around the edges. Push the stuffing in and glue down the remaining open edge (fig. 300). Gluing is not absolutely necessary, but is done to hold the pieces in place while sewing around them.

Fig. 300

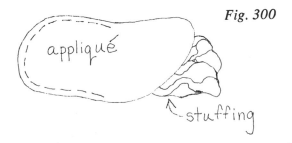

To stitch in the middle of padded areas, do the stitching before stuffing it. If you can't push the stuffing in by hand use a pencil or another instrument which will reach that area. Use the longest stitch on your machine, and brown paper strips to protect the leather.

I padded the areas of my design which naturally bulge; thighs, arms, breasts, abdomen and pillow.

My backing piece was purposely left with its natural edge. You may want to square it off. Beads, fur and decorative stitching were added later. As much as possible was sewn by machine, especially since my design is very large (plate 104).

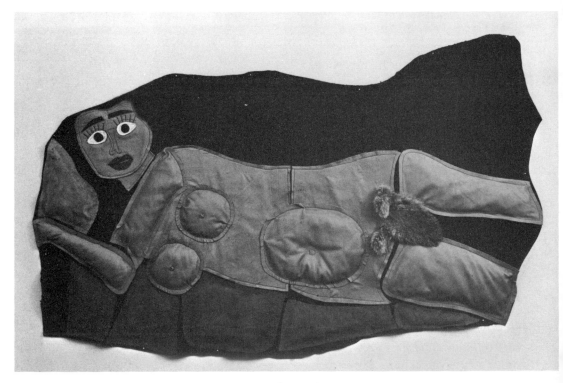

Plate 104

LEATHER SCULPTURE

Sculpture is generally defined as a three-dimensional work of art. It no longer has to stand by itself, but can be hung on a wall, suspended from a ceiling or supported by a separate base. Sometimes familiar objects such as chairs, empty bottles, and cans are used to support the material one is sculpting, and intentionally left recognizable, to be taken as part of the aesthetic appeal. Quite often a wide variety of materials are used to create a three-dimensional collage.

If you have had any experience with paper sculpture you'll find it helpful when sculpting with leather. The difference is that most leathers do not have the stiffness that most papers have. The main problem, then, is to make leather hold the form you want. Any way you devise to do this is acceptable. You can glue it to solid or firmer objects such as wood, cardboard or glass; work it over shapes made from crumpled paper, wire, wire mesh or plaster; stuff it with cotton batting or scraps; roll it into tubes; crumple it into balls or build up areas by layering.

When I begin any work of art I always have an idea how it will look when finished. Many people think that abstractions are easy to do, but those artists who are best at producing them, usually have a concrete understanding and mastery of realistic art. If you plan to work abstractly, you should first know the real form you are abstracting from.

Begin by gathering any objects and materials you have around the house which you think may be suitable to support the leather—empty bottles or boxes, rubber balls, beads, etc. Preliminary sketches may be made before beginning, to help solidify your ideas.

A bottle was used as the base for my sculpture. To begin, a thick coat of polymer gloss medium was brushed on the bottle. Scraps of leather were added while the medium was still wet, and pinched to create wrinkles or a veined effect. (Polymer gloss medium was used as glue for this entire sculpture). If you use it, check the bottle to be sure it is labeled to be used as a glue.

Areas around the bottom and middle were built up in layers by cutting each succeeding piece slightly smaller than the one preceding it and gluing the smaller pieces on top of the larger ones (fig. 301).

LAYERING

Fig. 301

top view   side view

To make major changes in the upper half of the base, cut a piece of cardboard to the desired shape. This one was rolled into a tube and taped to hold its shape. It was then stuffed with newspaper; taped in place on the bottle and covered with leather (fig. 302). To round off and cover the edges, tabs were cut and glued overlapping each other.

Tubes were made by rolling strips of varied widths. To keep them tightly rolled, gloss medium was put on the entire wrong side of each piece as it was rolled. Tabs for gluing can be made by cutting off all except 1½-inches of its length to a ½-inch depth. Clip this 1½-inch unglued area and spread it out to provide added strength when gluing (figs. 303 and 304).

The top piece is a strip of cardboard covered on both sides with leather. Faces were painted on before attaching the piece. The hair serves as tabs to hold it in place. The hand shapes were cut from cardboard and leather was glued to both sides (fig. 305).

Final touches were added with paint and bits of leather and suede. You might want to add materials like beads, feathers, aluminum foil or even use portions of photos for other interesting effects.

The leather was sealed with three coats of acrylic polymer matt varnish, which darkens the color slightly. Polymer medium not only stiffens or hardens many leathers, but it also curls it, if a stiff base is not used underneath. Test the polymer medium on scrap first to be sure you like the effect (plate 105).

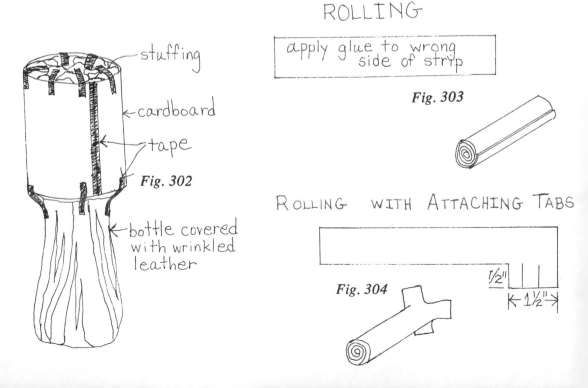

ROLLING

apply glue to wrong side of strip

Fig. 303

stuffing

cardboard

tape

Fig. 302

bottle covered with wrinkled leather

ROLLING WITH ATTACHING TABS

Fig. 304

½"

1½"

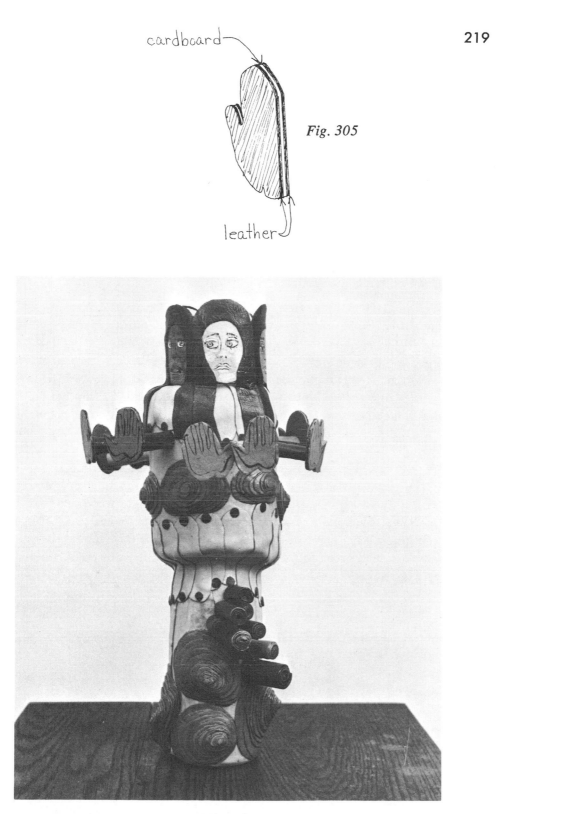

cardboard

Fig. 305

leather

Plate 105

OTHER SCULPTURE METHODS

One method of sculpting with leather has already been described along with ideas on how to embellish it. Following are other methods available to you.

    1. Mold and sew forms together (directions follow).

    2. Stuffed forms that are sewn together (fig. 306).

    3. Making solid shapes by gluing thick layers of leather together (directions follow). The leather can then be carved.

    4. Folding or bending leather.

    5. Making chicken wire frames and covering them with leather strips looped on, laced on, or glued on.

Molding Leather

While wet leather can be molded, stretched and shaped over other forms to create a new form, when it dries the leather will retain this new shape unless it is rewet and reshaped.

    Although there are many different procedures, a few basic steps are used with all. Four to eight-ounce vegetable tanned cowhide must be used. Immerse the leather in water until it is thoroughly wet. A little dish detergent will help the water penetrate the leather. It should take about 10 minutes. Squeeze the excess water out between two paper towels. Using one cf the following methods shape the leather over a form and let it dry for about two days. Do not take it off the form until it is absolutely dry.

    You could make a wood form by hand carving it or turning it on a lathe. But, it's easier to carve cork or styrofoam; use old wood salad bowls or, for some techniques, use ceramic and glass objects. When using objects like glass which are non-porous the leather must remain on the form longer because air will not get to the underside and it will dry slower. Whenever using nails, use the aluminum or galvanized kind because steel may stain the leather.

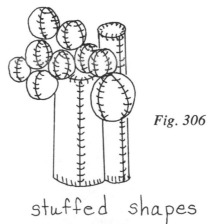

Fig. 306

stuffed shapes

One shape may not be enough to make the object you have in mind. By duplicating the same shape one or more times, you can join them together to create new forms. They can be stitched, laced, glued, riveted, or bound together.

MAKING A PLUG MOLD

1. Cut a shape from the middle of a ¾-inch plywood square with a jigsaw (fig. 307). The size of the square will be determined by the size of the item you're making. You will be left with two pieces.
2. Trim the plug ¼-inch all around to allow for the thickness of the leather (fig. 308). On both pieces sand all edges that will touch the leather (fig. 309).
3. Cover the cut from the edge of the wood with a brace (fig. 310).

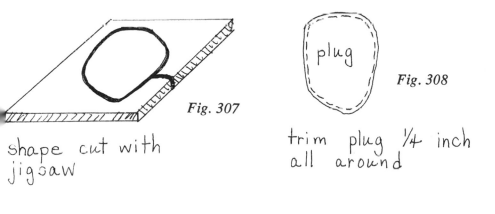

Fig. 307

shape cut with
jigsaw

plug

Fig. 308

trim plug ¼ inch
all around

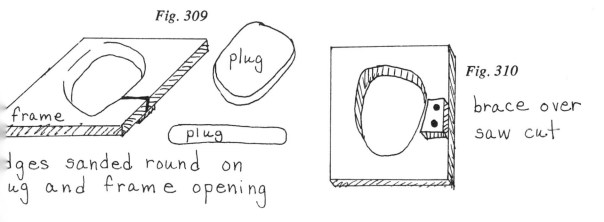

Fig. 309

frame

plug

plug

...dges sanded round on
...ug and frame opening

Fig. 310

brace over
saw cut

4. For deeper shapes, glue, nail or screw 2 or more layers of plywood together (fig. 311).

5. Soak the leather thoroughly. Place it over the hole and force the plug in (fig. 312). Be sure that the leather is stretched smooth on the side that will show. Let the leather dry thoroughly.

MAKING A ONE PIECE MOLD

1. Carve the basic shape from soft pine or any material that will hold nails (fig. 313).

2. Stretch the wet leather over this shape and nail in place. Do not hammer the nails all the way in, as they will be impossible to remove later. Place the nails in the section of leather that will be cut away later, not in the section that will be seen on the finished item (fig. 314).

3. Let it dry thoroughly. When you remove it, cut the excess leather off.

4. This mold works very successfully when two of the same shape are made and laced or sewn together (fig. 315), or when many of the same shapes are made and then cut into odd shapes and put together.

It should be noted here that it is usually easier to work with a basic shape rather than to spend a lot of time and energy carving something elaborate. This way, you can always rewet a portion of it and reshape that later (fig. 316).

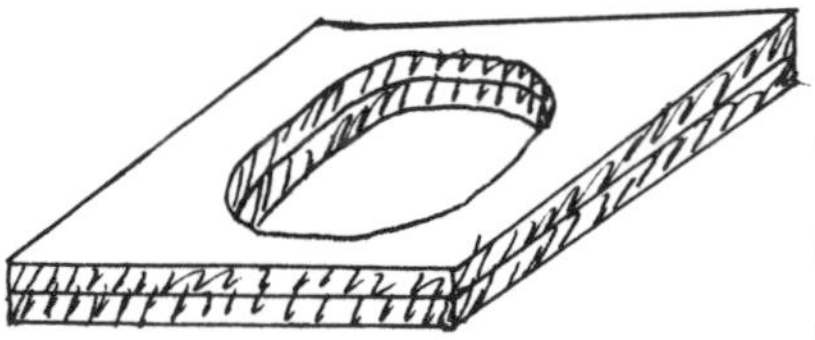

Fig. 311

two layers
of 3/4 inch
ply wood

plug

Fig. 312

plug forced into frame
with leather in between

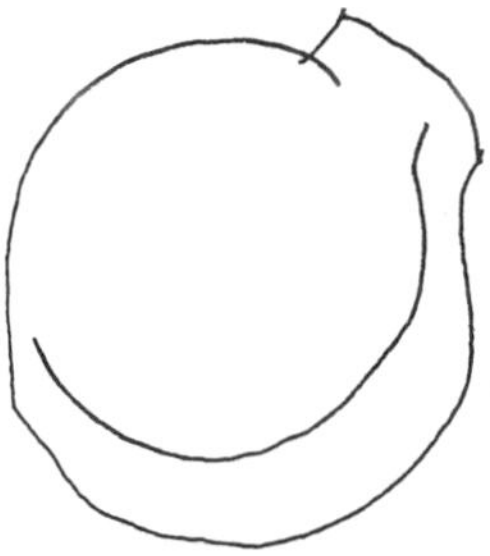

Fig. 314

Fig. 313

carved wood mold

wet leather stretched
and nailed over mold

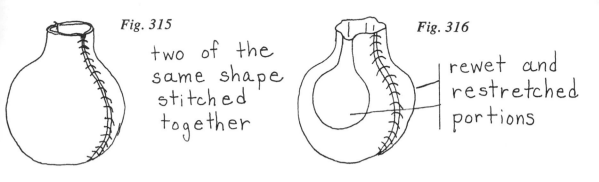

Fig. 315

two of the
same shape
stitched
together

Fig. 316

rewet and
restretched
portions

MAKING A TWO PIECE MOLD

1. Begin with two squares of ¾-inch plywood. Nail or glue the form to one piece (fig. 317). Cut a hole in the second piece ¼-inch larger all around than the form (fig. 318). Sand the edges smooth and round so that they will not damage the leather.

2. Place the wet leather over the form. Force the plywood piece with the hole over the leather. No nails are used. Hold these two pieces together with 4 C-clamps.

MAKING A MULTI-PIECE MOLD

1. Carve the shape to be molded, and glue or attach it to a plywood base (fig. 319).

2. Cut other shapes from thinner plywood (if you want to save a little on cost) to conform exactly to the outline of the shape outline you have just carved. These will fit all around it, like jigsaw pieces.

3. Stretch wet leather over the mold. Fit the pieces of plywood around the shape and nail them in place (fig. 320). Use a tool like a leather creaser to crease around the curves. This will help smooth out the leather.

4. Make at least two shapes and stitch or lace them together (fig. 321).

Fig. 317

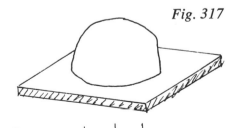

form glued to
plywood base

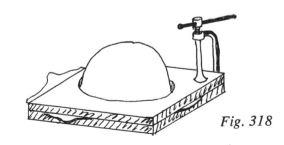

Fig. 318

top piece of plywood is
forced over wet leather —
place a C-clamp on
each corner

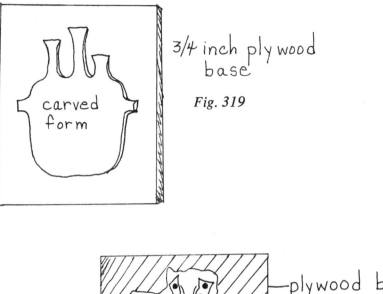

3/4 inch plywood
base

Fig. 319

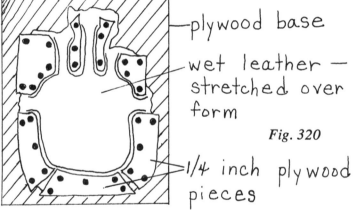

—plywood base

wet leather —
stretched over
form

Fig. 320

—1/4 inch plywood
pieces

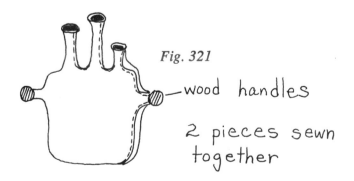

Fig. 321

—wood handles

2 pieces sewn
together

MAKING LEATHER INTO SOLID FORMS

Using vegetable-tanned cowhide, it's possible to make a solid block which can be carved like wood or to make solid forms such as boxes, and other shaped containers. How large your shape is depends on how ambitious you are. It can be as large as your piece or pieces of leather and as high as you wish to build it. The thicker your leather is the less work you'll have to do, but be sure that the leather is not so thick that it has a permanent bend in it and won't flatten out.

To make a solid form, many pieces must be glued one on top of the other. Before gluing rough up all surfaces that will be glued. This must be done to assure a strong bond. Use the strongest glue you can find; a wood contact glue. When the piece has dried, carve it with wood carving tools and gouges or whittle it with a knife. You can sand or burnish it smooth and paint or dye it (fig. 322).

The procedure for making a container is the same as for a solid with a few exceptions. First cut as many pieces of the same shape and size as you need to obtain the desired height. Cut out the same amount from the center of each one (fig. 323). For accuracy, cutting dies should be used (fig. 324), but it can be done with a compass and cut by hand. Cutting dies are simply big, single punches.

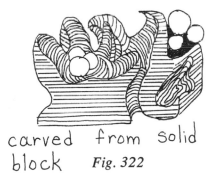

carved from solid
block *Fig. 322*

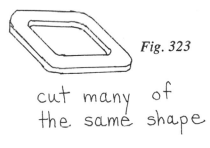

Fig. 323

cut many of
the same shape

cutting die

made with
large diameters

Fig. 324

Use one or more solid circles for the bottom of the container and one or more solid circles for the top. How many you glue together will depend on what you plan to do with it. If you plan to carve a deep design, you'll need more than one solid for the top. For a tight-fitting top, use one of the cut out centers glued to the underside of the top (fig. 325). Again, all surfaces to be glued together must be roughed first.

Glue together all the shapes with the cut out centers (fig. 326). Sand the inside of this construction before you glue it to the bottom piece.

If you don't plan to color the edges, apply beeswax to them and burnish by rubbing with one of the hand tools, as described in the section on thick leather, or if you do plan to apply coloring, simply wet the edges and burnish. All choppy edges will have a more finished look if polished; this can be done by hand or with an electric drill with a sanding drum attachment. After coloring, protect the surface by applying wax.

cover

Fig. 325

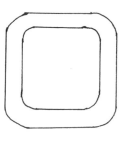

bottom view

side view

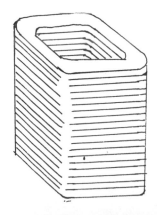

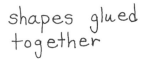

Fig. 326

shapes glued together

BURNT-AND-DYED LEATHER WALL HANGING

Burning a design on leather is similar to burning suede. Because this particular cut of leather was very thick it was possible to burn deep, dark lines without burning through. Whether you decide to do something pictorial or abstract, try to vary your shapes. By changing the pressure when applying the hot iron to the leather, you will get a variety of burnt tones.

MATERIALS

> Leather (used here: 24 x 30-inch chrome-tanned cowhide)
> Soldering iron
> Asbestos or a piece of cork
> Liquid dyes (used here: Rit yellow, gold, tangerine, evening blue, Kelly green, fuchsia)
> Sponge
> Brushes
> Water
> Dowel
> 3 metal rings
> Twine
> Revolving punch

Test your colors on a scrap first, trying them on dry or damp swatches. If you are going to use the damp method of application, dampen the area to be worked on with a sponge, dip your brush in water, then in dye and brush on. This method was used to get the light wash effect around the main shapes. Color was applied directly from the bottle (not diluted), to get darker, stronger tones. Some areas were rubbed with a damp sponge while still wet, purposely smearing the colors and thus carrying them over, as lighter tones, to other areas of the composition.

Cut a dowel appropriate for the size of your piece. Notch the ends of the dowel. Punch holes along the top edge of the leather and fit rings into them. Slip these rings onto the dowel. Tie each end of the string around the notches (plate 106).

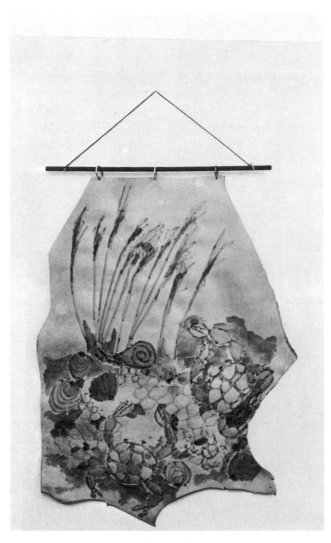

Plate 106

COLLAGE

Collage is a French word meaning "to paste a variety of things together to create an artistic composition." Anything you'd like to use on yours will add a personal touch to the final product.

MATERIALS

    Basket weaving reeds (used here: #4)
    Large piece of leather
    Smaller leather scraps
    Beads
    Rug yarn
    Embroidery thread
    Leather cement (a white glue, used here: Tite-bond)
    Mat board
    Ceiling tile
    Carpet tacks
    Scissors

MAKING THE FRAME

First decide on the overall shape you want. Working with flexible reeds allows great freedom of choice. Immerse your reeds in water and let them soak until thoroughly wet. While you're waiting for them to absorb the water, push carpet tacks into a ceiling tile in the shape you'd like for your frame. While the reeds are still wet, wind them around the tacks. Thong them together and let them dry (fig. 327).

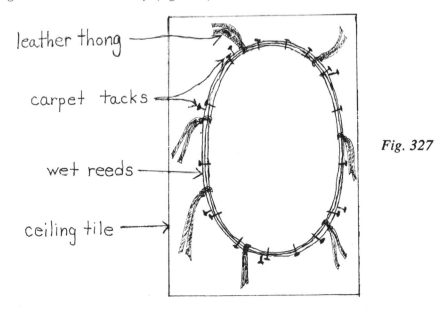

leather thong

carpet tacks

wet reeds

ceiling tile

Fig. 327

Fit your large leather piece in place without attaching it in any way. Slide a piece of mat board or heavy cardboard underneath. The cardboard will keep your frame from bending out of shape. If you can get heavier reeds, you may not need this cardboard backing. Trace around the frame shape and around any area of leather that doesn't cover the backing, if you have such an area. Cut off the excess mat board. Put the leather aside and glue the reed frame to this backing.

Once dry, refit the leather. Cut off the excess around the edges that are to be attached to the reed frame. Leave yourself at least 1½-inches on these edges (plate 107). Turn the leather wrong side up. Place the frame on top, wrong side up. Apply glue around the back edge of the mat board. Starting at the middle top and working down each side, ease the leather over the edge. Pull evenly as you go to fit the leather smoothly around the curve (fig. 328). If your entire piece is to be attached, leave the bottom half loose, so that you can get under the leather to sew. You can paste this portion of the edge later. Cut scrap pieces of leather and wool. Some pieces were used as found. Place all your materials in a design. Move them around until the design pleases you. In a composition of this sort, you'll find it more

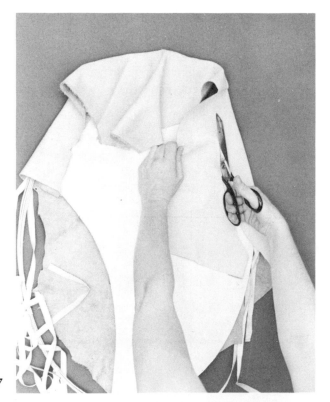

Plate 107

effective if at least a few of your pieces are touching or overlapping, rather than apart in little, separate islands. Of course, this is a simple way to create a successful work of art, which like all rules, has exceptions. If you have a great idea which requires separated pieces, by all means do it.

Two of the appliqué pieces and the beads were stitched on with doubled embroidery thread after being glued down. The rug wool was also glued down, but the overstitching was added for variety and strength. The loose rug wool was glued to the back and top edge and planned to fall exactly like you see it.

Punch a hole in your mat board, near the top edge and centered. Hammer a nail into the wall where it is to hang, and hook the hole onto the nail (plate 108).

leather cased around frame and glued

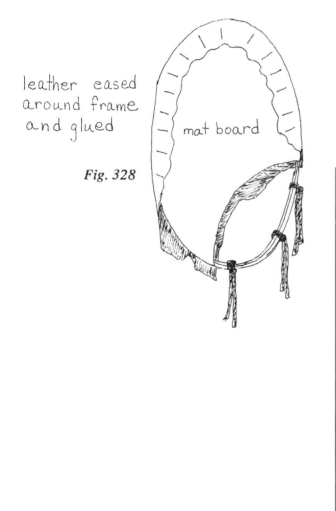

Fig. 328

Plate 108

SUEDE PAINTING

When I paint, I prefer to mix my paints directly on the canvas, rather than on a palette. Since acrylics dry fast, this technique has its drawbacks. It tends to eliminate much subtlety.

MATERIALS

Large piece of suede (used here: stiff split cowhide)
Acrylic paints
Polymer medium
Gel medium
Brushes
Canvas stretchers (same size as suede)
Carpet tacks (or upholstery tacks)
Ceiling tile (or other stiff board larger than the suede)

To begin, assemble the canvas stretchers. Cut your suede to fit this frame, slightly overlapping the wooden edge. Do not attach the suede to the stretchers. Now, tack your suede to the ceiling tile; stretch it out as evenly and as flat as possible. If you were to paint with your suede already attached to the stretchers, it would sag and stretch out of shape from the weight of the wet paint. Work with the acrylics as explained previously.

In this project, I painted the larger areas of color using the gel to thin the paint so it would flow on easily. A small amount of polymer medium was added to highlight certain areas, I brushed colors on at random around the figure, and used Polymer medium in varying amounts to create different tones. For the final step, I filled in and added outlines and darker areas by using colors straight from the tube. If you find that you have difficulty working with acrylics and need further help, there's an inexpensive booklet which can be purchased at your local art store. You'll also find a little practice and experimentation will be useful.

To finish, add picture hooks and wire (plate 109).

Plate 109

SCHOOL PROJECTS

Having once been a teacher myself, I realize the impossibility of being precise when setting down school projects. The teacher must take into account many things when planning her lesson—the age group, physical abilities, interests and supplies available. The items in this book will give the teacher a working knowledge of leather techniques. It is up to the teacher to adapt specific projects to her students.

Teachers can often obtain free scraps by going directly to a leather factory. But, with the stress on conservation and recycling, a good way to start a lesson would be to have the students collect old leather items to be cut apart and reused.

A study of animals, animal skins, and the history of clothing could lead into an art lesson, a social studies lesson or an ecology project.

Collages, either abstract or representational, are probably the best way to become acquainted with leather, and they can easily be adapted to almost any level. A collage does not have to be something to hang on a wall. It could also be something to hang around your neck.

SUGGESTIONS: Mini pictures, weaving, paper dolls (leather) and clothes, earrings, barrettes, necklaces, book covers, covered bottles or jars, doll clothes, decorative patches, bracelets, rings, amulets.

LEATHER AND SUEDE OLD AND NEW

As you work with, wear, and live with leather, you will begin to understand why man throughout the ages has chosen to adorn himself and his surroundings with it.

Leather keeps out the cold. It is generally sturdier than cloth, delightful to touch and to look at, and it gives one a general feeling of wellbeing.

We know that man, almost from the beginning, used animal skins for utilitarian reasons. One day he probably felt a chill and traded in his fig leaf for an animal pelt. The problem of sheer survival in primitive times left him little time to develop his imagination.

However, as people formed societies, introduced ritual and found leisure time, they created decorative leather items such as ceremonial masks and musical instruments (plates 110-112).

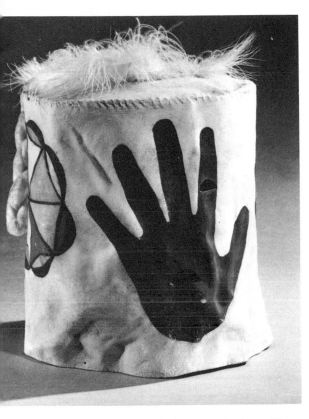

Plate 110. Anahoho Kachine mask from N. Mexico; of hide, paint, feathers and cotton. Courtesy of The Museum of Primitive Art.

Plate 111. Janus-faced mask from Nigeria, made of wood, skin and hair. Courtesy of The Museum of Primitive Art, New York.

Still later, man became dissatisfied with his personal effects. A plain old trunk was no longer good enough and craftsmen would spend weeks and months decorating one item (plate 113). Scenes of historical and religious events were embossed, cut into the leather and painted on objects. Leather was used to cover wood items and then gilded. Bone, mother-of-pearl, glass and other materials were used to create yet more intricate designs in decorating the piece, plate 114. Game boards, cabinets, jewel boxes, books and chairs were only a few of the items treated in this lavish way (plate 115).

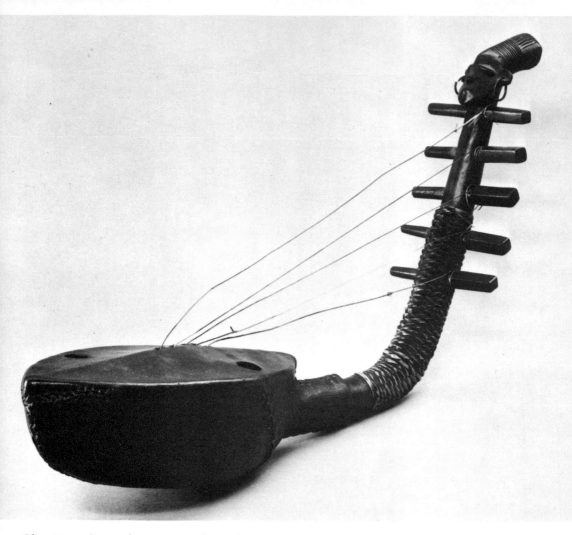

Plate 112.   Stringed instrument from the Congo made of leather, wood,
fiber and brass. Courtesy of The Museum of Primitive Art, New York.

(Opposite)
Plate 113.   French fifteenth century chest of brown leather, incised, em-
bossed and painted. Courtesy of The Metropolitan Museum of Art, Rogers
Fund, 1926.

(Opposite)
Plate 114.   Miniature cabinet of leather, wood, brass-gilt, bone, mother-of-
pearl and glass. Courtesy of The Metropolitan Museum of Art, New York.
Gift of Susan Bliss, 1948.

Plate 115. Spanish leatherwork checkers from the eighteenth century. Courtesy of The Metropolitan Museum of Art. Gift of Gustavus A. Pheiffer, 1948.

Walls were hung with decorated leather and man spent a great deal of time decorating the things he wore. Sixteenth, seventeenth and eighteenth century European aristocrats surrounded themselves with the most ornate and lavish items imaginable (plates 116-118).

Although there have been periods in America's history where decoration has been important, compared to seventeenth century Europe we were

(Opposite)
Plate 116. Spanish seventeenth century wall-hanging of leather, embossed, gilded and painted in colors. Courtesy of The Metropolitan Museum of Art. Gift of Lady Fitch, 1934.

(Opposite)
Plate 117. A pair of seventeenth century English gauntlets of buff leather with cuffs embroidered in silk and metal thread. Courtesy of The Metropolitan Museum of Art. Rogers Fund, 1928.

Plate 118.   French seventeenth century shoes of white kid, embroidered in silk. Courtesy of The Metropolitan Museum of Art. Rogers Fund, 1906.

a very subdued society. Not until recently have we begun to approach their lavishness, and to use leathers for anything other than luggage.

Items produced by craftsmen today are so varied that there's something to suit everyone's taste from very plain to very ornate.

What makes handmade items so great is the personal care involved, the pride in craftsmanship and the imaginative designs.

One modern day craftsman, Paul Venturini, spends a great deal of time working with the leather itself. His designs and decorations have clean simple lines. Molding hard leathers as well as suedes; neat, strong and durable methods of lacing and putting items together, and simple staining as well as sewing are his forte (plates 119-122).

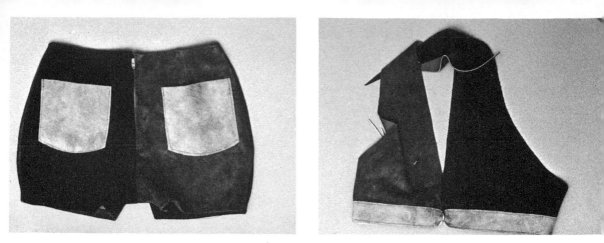

Plate 119.   Halter and Hot Pants of red, orange and navy cow-split suede, machine sewn. Created by Paul Venturini of Assingear Leather.

Plate 120.   Skirt of black, white and gray cabretta, machine sewn. Created by Paul Venturini of Assingear Leather.

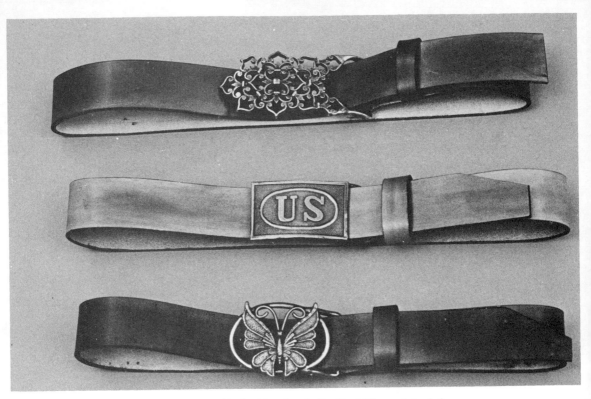

Plate 121.   Belts of stained cowhide. Handmade by Paul Venturini of Assingear Leather.

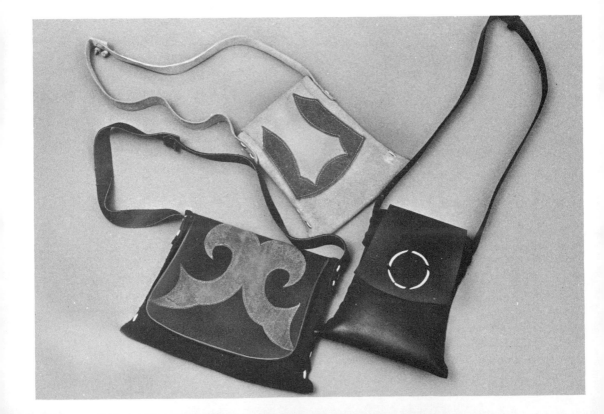

Others, like Linda Ardigo and Eileen Ferado work mostly with suedes. Their "Food Belts" are just a small indication of their ingenuity. What a little bit of suede and paint in the right hands can do! Linda also enjoys combining different materials and uses crocheting around suede to make charming feminine clothing (plates 123 and 124).

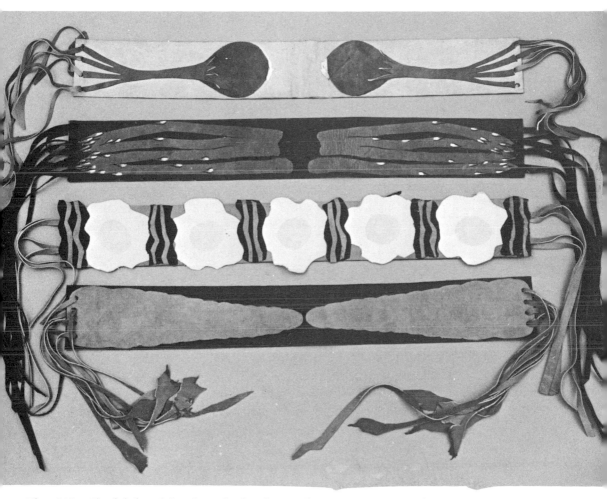

Plate 123. Food belts of Lamb suede, hand-painted in tempera. Created by Linda Ardigo and Eileen Ferado.

(Opposite)
Plate 122. Hand laced handbags with machine appliqué. The two on the left are suede cowhide and the one on the right is leather cowhide. Created by Paul Venturini of Assingear Leather.

Plate 12 4.   Created by Linda Ardigo

Ricky Schneider, Steve Goldenberg, Diane McNamara and Susan Maletich use the standard method for decorating leather, handtooling their items. Their final products though, are anything but standard. In their hands, tooling is a new and exciting art. They use a few different stamps and play around with them to get a great variety of effects. Some items are tooled and stained, others are tooled and hand-painted and still others are simply painted. Anything goes from a Porky Pig hair band (or bracelet if you prefer) to line designs, butterflies, or belts with a country scene (plates 125-127).

Plate 125. *Hand-tooled and hand-painted belts by Tinker Hill People.*

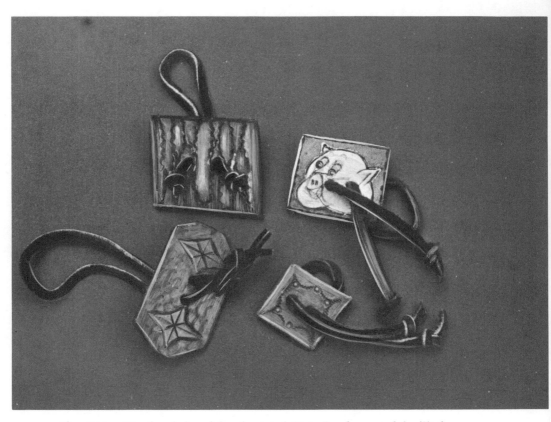

Plate 126. Hand-tooled and hand-painted Hair Bands created by Tinker Hill People.

As you can see, leathers can be handled in many different ways. Each artist adds his individuality to the piece he makes whether it is simple or intricate. What has been done in the past and what is being done now will give you ideas, not to copy, but to create new things all your own.

Today leather has once again been given an important place in our lives. Old methods, (like working with your own hands), can be used to make new and contemporary items.

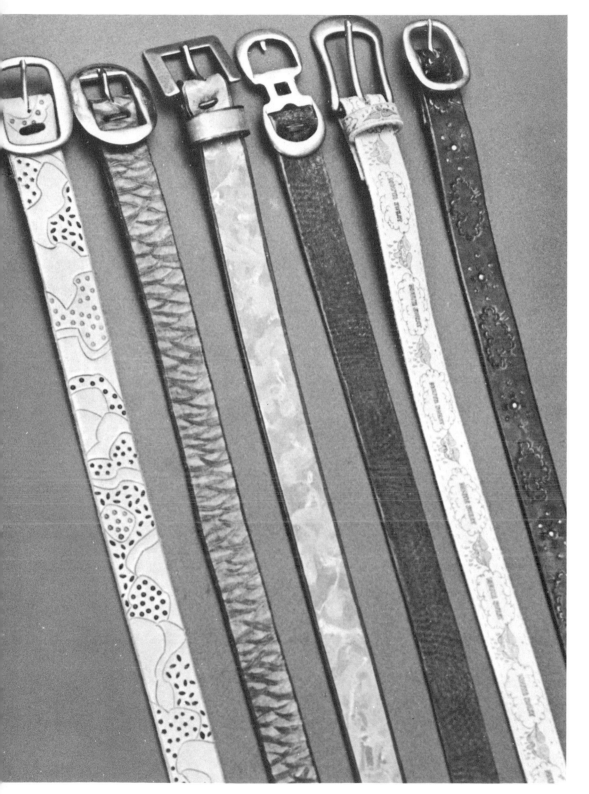

Plate 127.   Hand-tooled and hand-painted belts created by Tinker Hill People.

SOURCES OF SUPPLY

Art Handicrafts Co., 3512 Flatlands Ave., Brooklyn, N. Y. 11234: All leather supplies. Free catalog.

Leathercrafters Supply Co., 25 Great Jones St., New York, N. Y. 10012; Leather, fur, suede, tools, findings, dyes. Free catalog.

Louis Kaminsky and Sons, Inc., 134 W. 29th St., New York, N. Y. 10001; Old and New Furs.

Mac Leather Co., 424 Broome St., New York, N. Y. 10012; Leather, suede.

Ed Nitsos Furs Inc., 227 W. 29th St., New York, N. Y. 10001; Furs.

Pollacks Furriers Supply Corp., 160 W. 29th St., New York, N. Y. 10001: Fur, leather, linings, supplies.

Renar Leather Co., 68 Spring St., New York, N. Y. 10012: Leather and suede.

Skil-Crafts, P. O. Box 105, Joplin, Mo., 64801; All supplies.

Tandy Leather Co. Inc., 330 Fifth Ave., New York, N. Y. 10036: 1310 Mission St., San Francisco, Calif. 94103; 730 Commonwealth Ave., Boston, Mass. 02115; 3901 S. Main St., Houston, Texas 77002: All leather supplies; Mail order, free catalog.

Tinker Hill People (Eric Schneider, Steve Goldenberg, Diane McNamara, Susan Meletich): Tinker Hill Road, R.F.D. #3, Putnam Valley, N. Y. 10579: Handmade leather items.

Paul A. Venturini, Assingear Leather, 607 George Road, Cliffside Park, N. J. 07010. Handmade leather items.

Veteran Leather Co., Inc., 729 Broadway, New York, N. Y. 10003: Suede and leather, tools, findings. Free catalog.

Also refer to classified telephone directory pages under Leather, Leather Findings, Leather Scrap, Hobby Shops, Arts and Crafts Supplies, Notions (for eyelets, needles, etc.).

INDEX